HOUSE PLANTS

HOUSE PLANTS

A Complete Book on Plant Care

With Photographs by Bill Swan

New York Botanical Garden

Banner Press   New York, New York

Managing Editor   Linda Timko Gonzalez
Illustrator   Maureen Marsh
Photographs (Pages 33-96)   Bill Swan

CONTENTS

Apartment Gardening

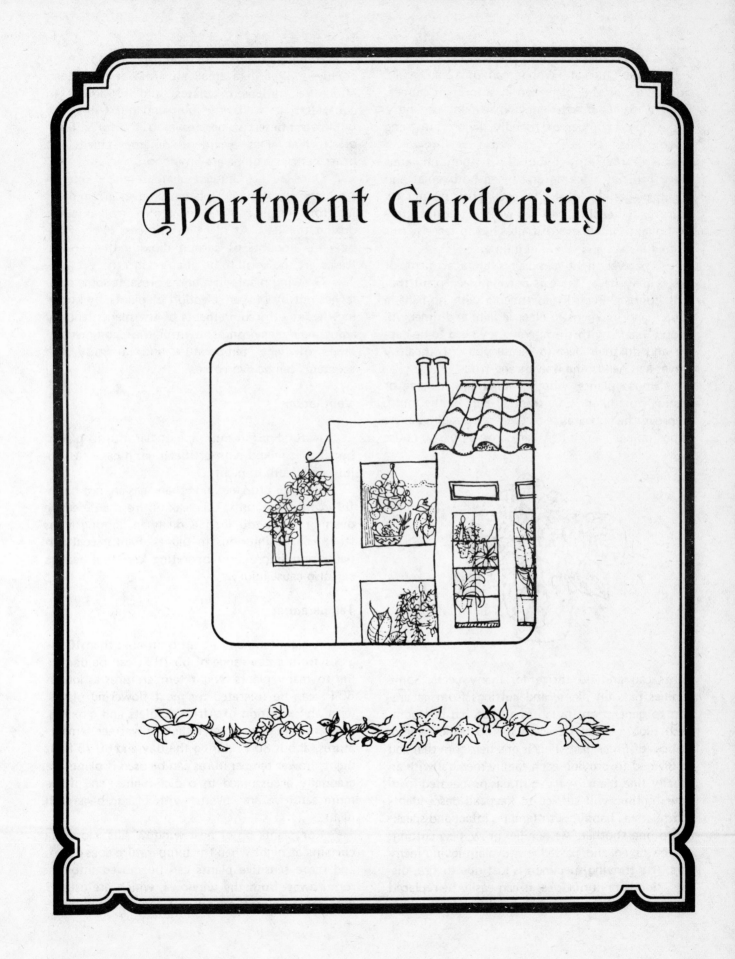

City dwellers with limited opportunities to walk in the fields and woods, can, on a small scale, bring part of the plant world into their homes. Even a compact efficiency apartment can be a home for a number of friendly, living, breathing green plants.

Requiring a minimum of attention, no veterinary care, no walking and being both quiet and clean, plants are ideal city pets. They do not require daily feeding, and self-watering devices may be bought which make it possible to leave plants alone for days and weeks at a time.

Whatever light exposures an apartment or house may have, there is a living green plant that will flourish. Even in apartments with no light, a simple and inexpensive electric light and timer will supply plants with the energy they need to be happy and do their best to please you with healthy leaves and handsome flowers and fruits.

House plants, whether climbing, hanging or resting quietly in some tranquil part of the room, improve the appearance of their surroundings as no other object can. When cared for properly, house

plants can and do thrive for many years. Some families pass on plants and cuttings from generation to generation, much as a treasured heirloom. Each bloom is an occasion for nostalgic remembrances of times past. This is one heirloom that can be divided to provide each family member with an equally fine plant. A few cuttings propagated from time to time will suffice to keep all descendants and relatives happy, with families intact and speaking to one another. As families grow, new cuttings can be taken and passed on to plant-loving members. If a thriving specimen is lost due to fire, disease, floods or tornadoes, it can easily be replaced with little expense and no heartaches.

Home gardening offers an opportunity for a creative outlet in a small area and at little cost. Miniature gardens in plates, and terrariums in aquariums, as well as in pint and quart jars, can duplicate a desert scene, a swamp, the forest floor or a formal Japanese garden. Tomatoes, chives, and other herbs can all be grown indoors.

Once people thought plants removed oxygen from the air. Actually, plants remove carbon dioxide from the air and add oxygen in small amounts during the day. At night the process is reversed, but the amounts of carbon dioxide that are released are too small to be of any concern.

Growing plants in a home presents some challenges but by proper selection of plants, by knowing the growth requirements of the plants, and by adjusting the environment within the recommended limits of light, temperature and humidity, the problems can be overcome.

Ventilation

Natural gas, if pure, is not harmful to plants, but if it is mixed with artificial gas it can cause injury and death to plants.

Butane, propane and ethane gas are not harmful in trace amounts. Gas leaking from a defective oven or from too long a delay in lighting a gas stove can be injurious to plants. Faulty coal furnaces and improperly operating kerosene heaters can also cause injury.

Temperature

A night temperature drop of more than 10 degrees from a day range of 65-70°F. can be damaging to many plants. Night temperatures as low as 50°F. can be tolerated by most flowering plants, with an exception of African violets and gloxinia. Most foliage plants prefer slightly warmer temperatures, about 80°F. during the day and 60-75°F. at night. Lower temperatures can be used if plants are gradually accustomed to cooler nights, and if the more sensitive are covered with plastic bags each night.

For plants on or near window sills, close the curtains at night when the temperature goes down, and more sensitive plants can be moved into the room away from the windows, which are usually cold spots unless there are storm windows in place.

Never place plants in front of or above heat outlets in the cool season, or air conditioners during summer, as the blasts of air are harmful, increasing water loss and dehydration among other damages.

Plants recommended for offices

The temperature in offices varies, especially during the evening and on weekends. The light is usually poor and plants are often placed near drafty locations such as windows, doors and heat outlets, so offices do indeed require special plants that can withstand these conditions.

aralia	jade plant
Chinese evergreen	Norfolk Island pine
dracaena	philodendron
dumb cane	pothos
fig	spathiphylum

Light

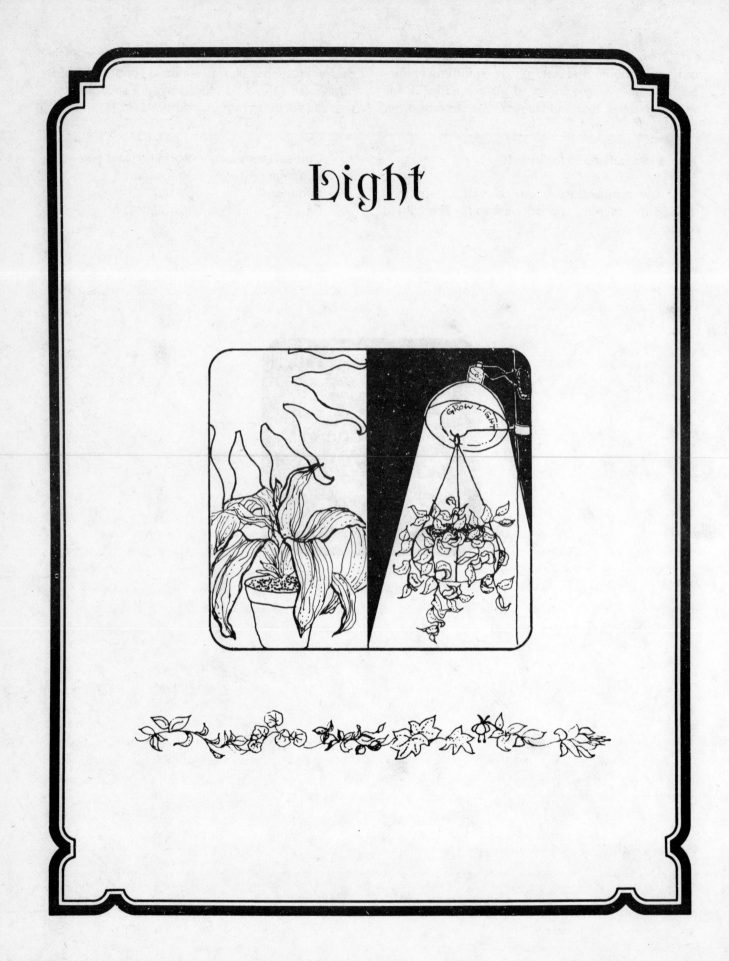

This chapter is one of the most important in the book. Adequate light is the absolutely indispensable factor in growing plants in the home.

Without sunlight, or an acceptable substitute, green plants cannot manufacture the food they need to grow and survive and they soon die.

If sunlight is low in intensity, or lacking, in a part of the home or office, a supplemental light source is required.

Different kinds of plants require varying amounts of light to grow well. These requirements are not strictly inflexible but will vary with room temperature, water and humidity and the age of the plants. Flowering plants, cacti and succulents generally require higher light quantities than do foliage plants.

To measure light, a very inexpensive light meter is useful in determining light in foot candles. The upper scale measures light in lux units when the knob at the lower right is set at x. Multiply the reading on the upper dial by 10 to give you foot candles, the common unit of measurement used for plants. This handy little meter also measures temperatures in F°. on the lower scale.

The table provides a guide to the amount of light commonly found at different exposures under a range of conditions as measured at noon on a bright, sunny day, by standing where the plant will be placed, and pointing the meter at the light source. Knowing the exposure you plan on using and the approximate available light means you can select plants adapted to that particular light situa-

GUIDE TO LIGHT EXPOSURES

Low Light 50- to 150-foot candles

North window exposure
In front of the window with most of the sky blocked.
3 to 5 feet back from, or on either side, with a clear view of the sky.

East or west window exposures
3 to 5 feet back from the window with most of the sky blocked.
6 to 10 feet back from the window with a clear view of the sky.

South window exposures
Up to 10 feet back from, or 3 to 5 feet on either side of, the window with most of the sky blocked.
Up to 15 or 20 feet back from, or 5 to 8 feet on either side of, the window with a clear view of the sky.

Medium Light 150- to 200-foot candles

North window exposure
Directly in front of the window with a clear view of the sky.

East or west window exposure
Directly in front of the window with about half of the sky blocked from view.
3 to 5 feet from, or just to either side of, the window with a clear view of the sky.

South window exposure
Up to 10 feet back from, or 2 to 3 feet on either side of, the window with a clear view of sky.

High Light 200- to 450-foot candles

East or west window exposure
Directly in front of the window with a clear view of the sky.

South window exposure
Directly in front of the window with about half of the sky blocked from view.
Up to 5 feet back from, or just to either side of, with a clear view of the sky.

Direct Light 1000- to 1500-foot candles

This would be a category providing direct sunlight unimpeded by curtains or barriers, usually a south window exposure.

tion, giving you a good start in successful home gardening.

This light meter measures light in lux units when the knob at the lower right is set at "x." Multiply the reading by 10 to get foot candles. The lower scale measures temperatures in degrees Fahrenheit.

If possible, consider rotating plants every week or so to provide light to all sides as an aid to uniform growth.

In summary we note that many plants will thrive in direct sunlight, including the artillery plant, cacti, Christmas cactus, geranium, kalanchoe, snake plant and stonecrop. South exposure, or east or west exposures receiving several hours of sunlight, are suitable for this class of plants.

Shade tolerant plants are usually foliage species grown for the beauty of their leaves. Included in this category are the dumb cane, Chinese evergreen, fiddleleaf fig, grape ivy, peperomia, philodendron, rubber plant and snake plant. All are well suited for northern exposure with poor, weak light.

Partial shade plants include flowering as well as foliage species such as African violet, Boston fern, caladium, and croton which need somewhat more light than the shade tolerant plants.

SUNLIGHT SUBSTITUTES

Incandescent light

Electric light can be used partially or entirely to substitute for sunlight; the equipment needed can range from a gooseneck desk lamp with a 75-watt bulb to combinations of incandescent bulbs and fluorescent tubes.

Incandescent bulbs of the kind we all use at home, frosted or clear, are satisfactory for growing plants indoors. They are inexpensive and their color composition is very close to sunlight, strong in blues and reds. Their biggest drawbacks are the high amount of heat they generate and the irrelatively short life span. They can be used with a reflector or in some cases bought with a built-in reflector.

150-watt PAR-38 projection lamps can be placed 8 to 10 feet above foliage plants for best results. A 150-watt incandescent lamp, with reflector, can be used on shorter foliage plants, placed about 6 feet away.

Fluorescent light

Much in use are a wide variety of fluorescent tubes. They produce more light with less heat and have a much longer life span than the incandescent bulbs. There are a number of fine fluorescent tubes available for indoor plant growing. Here, by brand name, are a few that can be used with excellent results:

General Electric
Daylight
Cool white
Plant light

Duro-Test
Vita-Lite

Sylvania
Gro-Lux
Wide spectrum Gro-Lux

Westinghouse
Plant-Gro
Agrolite

All fluorescent tubes must go into the correct fixture or ballast; 40 watt tubes are well suited for most home gardening. For some plants needing higher light intensities, the use of incandescent bulbs in combination with fluorescent tubes is recommended, with about 1 out of each 5 watts provided by the incandescent bulb. Thus, if you used a double bank of fluorescent 40-watt tubes, a total of 80 watts, 14 to 20 watts of incandescent bulbs would be fine.

Fixtures

White reflectors for fluorescent tubes are recommended to reflect the maximum of light onto the plants.

The standard two-tube fixtures, easily found at discount and hardware stores, are ideal. The 4-foot, rapid-start lamps are recommended because they are economical to operate. The cost of one two-lamp fixture with two 40-watt bulbs for a 14-hour day, would be less than five cents a day, if the rate was three cents per kilowatt hour.

Light gardens

There are several small tabletop electric gar-

dens on the market at garden stores. Some models come assembled and will fit on a coffee table or tabletop.

For the home gardener who might want to assemble a range of fixtures to go with the decor of a room or area, shown are three sets of plants and photos.

Vacation lights

When on vacation, leave plants in subdued light, usually out of direct sunlight. However, if you plan on being gone for an extended length of time, some light supplement is needed. Use a timing device that turns the lights on at a pre-selected time and turns them off at a pre-selected time. If you are using incandescent bulbs be sure they are not too close to the plant as they can cause burning.

Incandescent bulbs can be used during the winter as a protection against unexpected night temperature drops. Time them to go on at night and off during the day.

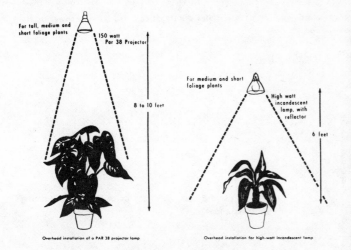

For foliage plants, place a 150-watt PAR-38 projection lamp 8 to 10 feet away from the plant. (Left) For shorter foliage plants, place a 150-watt incandescent bulb with reflector six feet above the plant.

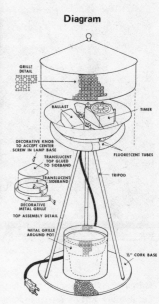

A free-standing, round light garden can be a decorative addition to the home, as well as providing additional light for plants.

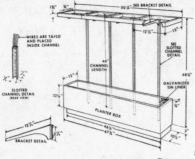

Diagram

This planter is large enough to hold taller plants. It can also be effectively used as a room divider.

Diagram

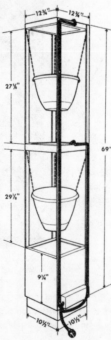

Timers can be used to turn lights on and off during your absences.

This vertical indoor planter is specifically designed to successfully culture plants in hanging baskets.

REQUIREMENTS FOR SELECTED HOUSE PLANTS

Temperature

cool = 40-60°F.
medium = 60-65°F.
warm = above 65°F.

Watering

Dry—These should dry out between waterings and need watering only every 1½-2 weeks. If watered too often the plants will probably lose their leaves and the roots may rot.

Medium—These need watering every 3-7 days. These plants will also be damaged if allowed to dry out. Do not water too often since this would cause too rapid growth as well as possible damage to the plant.

Moist—Water every other day. These would be damaged if allowed to dry out. They are not kept moist to the touch but rather are kept to the same degree of moistness at all times.

LOW LIGHT

Plant	Water	Temperature	Mature Plant Size
ferns	moist	warm	pot, floor
gold dust plant, *Aucuba japonica "variegata"*	moist	cool to medium	tree, floor plant
palms	moist	warm	pot, tree, floor
spindletree, *Euonymus* spp.	moist	medium	pot

MEDIUM LIGHT

Plant	Water	Temperature	Mature Plant Size
achimenes, *Achimenes* spp.	moist	medium	pot
caladium, *Caladium bicolor*	moist	warm	pot
calathea, *Calathea* spp.	moist	warm	pot
cape cowslip, *Lachenalia* spp.	medium	cool	pot
cape primrose, *Streptocarpus* spp.	moist	medium	pot
cast iron plant, *Aspidistra lurida*	medium	cool to medium	pot
Chinese evergreen, *Aglaonema* spp.	dry	warm	pot
cineraria, *Senecio cruentus*, and German ivy, *Senecio mikanioides*	moist	cool	pot
cissus, *Cissus* spp.	moist	medium	pot
columnea, *Columnea* spp.	moist	medium	pot
crossandra, *Crossandra* spp.	moist	warm	pot
dracaena, *Dracaena* spp.	dry to medium	medium	pot, floor
dumb cane, *Dieffenbachia* spp.	dry to medium	medium	pot, floor
dwarf boxwood, *Buxus sempervirens*	moist	medium	pot
fat lizzie, *Fatshedera lizei*	moist	cool	pot
fig, *Ficus* spp.	moist	medium	floor, pot, tree
flame violet, *Episcia* spp.	moist	warm	pot
flamingo flower, *Anthurium* spp.	moist	medium	pot
fuchsia, *Fuchsia* spp.	moist	medium	pot
Japanese aralia, *Fatsia japonica*	moist	cool	floor, pot
nephtytis, *Syngonium podophyllum*	dry	warm	pot
peperomia, *Peperomia* spp.	medium	medium	pot
philodendron, *Philodendron* spp., some will tolerate less light	dry to medium	warm	tree, floor, pot
pilea, *Pilea* spp.	moist	medium	pot, floor
pothos, *Scindapsus aureus*	moist	medium to warm	pot
pouch flower, *Calceolaria* spp.	medium	cool	pot
purple waffle plant, *Hemigraphis exotica*	medium	medium	pot
seersucker plant, *Geogenanthus undatus*	moist	warm	pot
shamrock, *Oxalis* spp.	medium	medium	pot
silvervein fittonia, *Fittonia verschaffelti argyroneura*	moist	warm	pot
snake plant, *Sansevieria* spp.	dry	warm	pot
spider aralia, *Dizygotheca elegantissima*	moist	warm	floor, pot
spider plant, *Chlorophytum capense*	moist	warm	pot

Plant	Water	Temperature	Mature Plant Size
strawberry geranium, *Saxifraga sarmentosa*	medium	cool	pot
three men in a boat, *Rhoeo discolor*	moist	medium	pot
ti plant, *Coryline terminalis*	moist	medium	pot
Transvaal daisy, *Gerbera jamesoni*	medium	warm	pot
wax plant, *Hoya carnosa*	medium	medium	pot

HIGH LIGHT

Plant	Water	Temperature	Mature Plant Size
African violet, *Saintpaulia* spp.	moist	warm	pot
aphelandra, *Aphelandra* spp.	moist	warm	pot
aralia, *Polyscias* spp.	moist	warm	floor, pot
azalea, *Rhododendron* spp.	moist	cool	pot
baby tears, *Helxine soleiroli*	medium	cool	pot
beefstock plant, *Iresine* spp.	moist	cool to medium	pot
begonia, *Begonia* spp.	moist	warm	pot
calla lily, *Zantedschia aethiopica*	moist	medium	pot
chocolate plant, *Pseudcranathemum alatum*	medium	medium	pot
Christmas cactus, *Zygocactus truncatus*	medium	cool	pot
chrysanthemum, *Chrysanthemum* spp.	moist	medium to warm	pot
cyclamen, *Cyclamen* spp.	moist	cool	pot
Easter lily, *Lilium longiflorum*	moist	medium	pot
English ivy, *Hedera helix*	moist	cool	pot
fairy rose, *Rose chinensis minima*	moist	warm	pot
geranium, *Pelargonium* spp.	medium	cool	pot
gloxinia, *Sinningia speciosa*	moist	warm	pot
Japanese aralia, *Fatsia japonica*	moist	medium	floor, pot
Jerusalem cherry, *Solanum pseudo-capsicum*	moist	cool	pot
Kenilworth ivy, *Cymbalaria muralis*	moist	cool to medium	pot
lantana, *Lantana camara*	moist	warm	pot
marigold, *Calendula* spp.	dry to medium	cool to medium	pot
mock orange, *Pittosporum tobira*	moist	cool	floor, pot
Norfolk Island pine, *Araucaria excelsa*	moist to medium	cool	tree, floor, pot
oleander, *Nerium oleander*	moist	medium	pot
ornamental pepper, *Capsicum frutescens*	medium	cool	pot
podocarpus, *Podocarpus macrophylla*	dry to medium	cool	floor, tree, pot
poinsettia, *Euphorbia pulcherrima*	medium	medium	pot
prayer plant, *Maranta* spp.	moist	warm	pot
primrose, *Primula obconia, P. malacoides*	medium	medium	pot
schefflera, *Schefflera actinophylla*	dry to medium	cool to medium	tree, floor, pot
screwpine, *Pandanus veitchi*	moist	warm	pot
spathiphylum, *Spathiphylum clevelandi*	moist	medium	pot
succulents and cactus	medium	warm	pot
velvet plant, *Gynura aurantiaca*	moist	medium	pot
wandering Jew, *Tradescantia fluminensis,* and *Zebrina pendula*	moist	warm	pot

DIRECT LIGHT

Plant	Water	Temperature	Mature Plant Size
amaryllis *Amaryllis* spp.	moist	medium to warm	pot
calamondin orange, *Citrus mitis*	dry	warm	pot
citrus other than calamondin, *Citrus* spp.	moist	warm	floor, tree, pot
coleus, *Coleus* spp.	moist	cool	pot
croton, *Codiaeum variegatum*	moist	warm	pot
gardenia, *Gardenia* spp.	moist	medium	pot
hibiscus, *Hibiscus rosen-sinensis*	moist	warm	pot
impatiens, *Impatiens* spp.	moist	warm	pot

Feeding and Watering

Both fertilizing and watering are as much an art as a science. A sensitivity to the appearance of your plants and a knowledge of how they look when well fed and watered is really the basis of a fruitful program.

Fertilizer

A look at the fertilizer shelf in a garden shop can be startling. A walk to a nearby garden center can reveal several package fertilizers intended for the same type of plant, for instance, roses. One may be labelled 11-6-4, another 10-7-5 and a third 6-10-4. How in the world does one decide which to use? Which formula is best?

First, let us see what the formula, the three numbers, really mean.

Nitrogen-N

The first number is a percent figure for nitrogen (N). 10 means 10 percent, or 10 pounds of nitrogen per 100 pounds of fertilizer. Nitrogen is essential to vegetative growth, that is, the parts of the plant above ground. When N is deficient, plant growth is stunted and the foliage turns a pale yellow. However, too much nitrogen can push the plant into an extreme vegetative stage and reduce or totally inhibit flowering. Such plants are weak and very dark green.

In the broadest term more nitrogen is needed for young plants making their first growth and for plants beginning seasonal growth prior to flowering. Less nitrogen is needed as plants flower and then die back.

Phosphorus-P

The second number in the formula refers to the percentage of phosphorus. This nutrient is important to proper root growth, flowering and fruiting.

Too much phosphorus can increase flower production at the cost of a stunted plant. Too little phosphorus causes plants to be slow to flower and seed and fruits are dwarfed. Phosphorus is needed for best flowering. Some plants demonstrate a reddish-purple foliage color when phosphorus is deficient.

Potassium-K

The third number refers to potassium whose role is not quite so clear cut as the first two. One of the functions of potassium in a plant is to lessen the tendency to wilting due to water loss from the plant. K also plays a role in strengthening stems and is involved to some extent in providing resistance to insects and certain fungus diseases.

Feeding

If you use a good rich soil when potting you do not need any fertilizer for three or four months or until the plants have become established and the root system begins to grow! Do not fertilize dormant plants nor newly purchased plants in flower. Growing plants may need fertilizer every six to ten weeks.

By far the easiest way to fertilize potted plants is with the liquid form whether bought that way or mixed by you. If you use an already mixed liquid form, follow the directions. If you mix your own, select a low analysis fertilizer such as 5-10-5 or a 4-12-4. Dissolve a teaspoon in a quart of warm but not hot water, stir well and allow to stand overnight.

Apply the fertilizer solution during the growing period at intervals of six to ten weeks, applying enough each time to wet the soil thoroughly.

Low analysis dry fertilizers can be used, particularly if they are of the slow release type. But never, never apply liquid or dry fertilizer to dry soil or severe root damage may result.

Special comments

Acid loving plants such as azaleas, camellias and gardenias lose their bright green foliage color if the soil is too alkaline. This condition is called *chlorosis,* or lack of color. The problem can be handled by adding a small amount of cholated iron to the pot, or a little powdered sulfur once a year. The iron remedies the chlorosis and the sulfur remedies the cause, alkalinity.

As with our other house pets, dogs and cats, in house plants overeating is much more of a problem than undereating. Over-fertilizing can cause burned looking leaf margins, very heavy vegetative growth and in extreme cases, death.

Watering

Amounts

The plant's need for water will depend on its age, size, vigor, room temperature, light exposure and humidity in the air.

A successful plantsperson will quickly learn to read the condition of the plant and soil to know if watering is called for. A wilting plant in the morning is a warning of water need. Wilting between noon and 3:00 p.m. is not too significant as at that time increased light intensity as well as higher temperatures result in greater water loss from plants.

Usually a plant needs water when the soil surface appears "dry." Many soils look lighter in color when drying occurs. Dark colored soils do not show this color difference. Feeling the soil will serve to tell you if water is needed.

Never, never use cold water, but use water that is close to room temperature. The time of day is not of any importance, but a good many people prefer to water in the morning, probably more for their convenience than the plant's benefit.

Overwatering can result in rotting roots.

Applying water

Watering from below is much preferred because there is no chance of washing soil away from the plant stem. It also makes it easier to know when the soil is wet through. The simplest way to water from below is to stand the pots in a container with 2 or 3 inches of water and wait until the surface becomes damp before removing the pots.

A very practical and inexpensive self-watering device can be made using a wick to move water up into the soil. Take a 6 or 9 inch length of wick and pass it through the drainage hole, unravel it and cover the bottom of the pot with it. Then replace the soil leaving out the coarse drainage material at the bottom of the pot. Pack the soil down with your fingers to insure contact between wick and soil.

Next, with about 2 to 3 inches of wick extending from below, place the pot in a container of water, 2 to 3 inches deep. If the water is too deep and the soil gets too wet, lower the water level. If the soil remains too dry, raise the water level. Be sure to keep water in the reservoir. If the soil becomes too dry, half submerge the pot in water for 30 minutes, then put it back into the reservoir refilled to its proper level.

This method keeps the soil moist continuously which is not always needed. By all means avoid this method with cacti and plants you are drying out to go into the rest period.

About once a month flush the pots that are using the wick method, by watering them thoroughly from the top to wash out any excess fertilizer salts which may have accumulated. The water that drains out of the drainage hole should be considered waste water.

Misting plants can be done with a little rubber bulb sprayer.

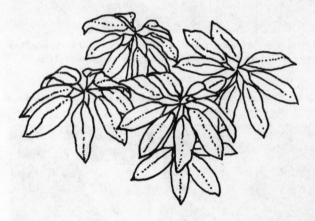

Vacation watering

If you find it necessary to leave your plants from time to time, you may wonder what to do with your plants while you are gone. There are a number of systems that can be established and combined, depending on how long you will be gone.

For vacations of up to two weeks there is a little device which can be very helpful. It is a plastic reservoir that is filled with water and buried in the soil. A flow retarder at the top slows down the water flow. With the retarder in position water lasts for an average of fifteen and a half days when used with a flowering geranium in a 5-inch plastic pot. Without the retarder, water flow is greater and the reservoir will empty in an average of ten days.

Double potting can be useful during absences from home as well as at other times. This method simply uses two pots, one inside the other, with damp sphagnum moss in between the two pots. The inner pot should be of porous material like

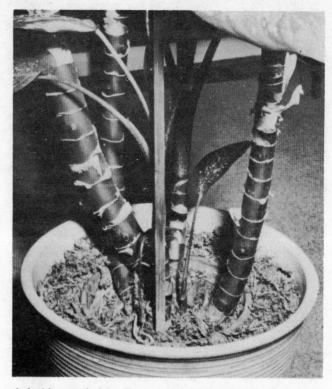

This is how the wick should look before you put soil in the pot. The other end of the wick should be placed in a container of water.

A plant can be covered with a plastic bag to keep it from drying out while you are on vacation.

A double-potted plant. The inner pot is clay; the outer pot is filled with peat moss.

The bulb contains a reservoir of water which will water the plant automatically.

The end of the plastic tube is plugged. Notice the row of holes along the tube. Fill the tube with sand, and then with water.

clay, the outer one of non-porous material. The outer pot does not need a drainage hole. It is important to allow an inch or two between the sides and bottoms of the pots.

Another method good for about five to eight days is to water your plant well, then cover it with a plastic bag to reduce water loss. If the pot is clay or other porous material cover it to minimize water loss too.

For a long weekend you can keep a plant moist by using plastic tubing an inch in diameter. Plug the bottom end with cork or a bit of plastic held in place with a rubber band. Drill 1/8-inch holes up and down the tube every half inch, vertically in four rows. Put the tube into the pot, fill it with sand and then fill with water.

Pots for Plants

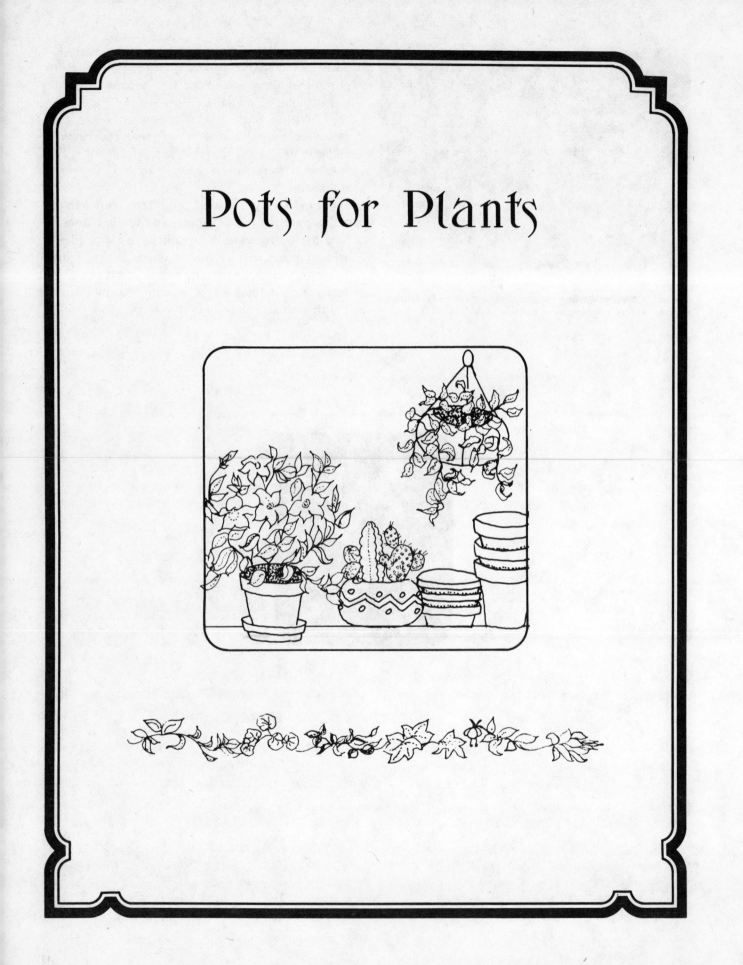

Plants can be grown in just about any kind of container if provision is made for drainage. Even if no drainage takes place through drainage holes or porous walls, plants can be grown with an inch or two of pebbles or gravel at the bottom of the container. Watertight pots, however, are troublesome as any excess water will collect at the bottom of the pot and damage plant roots.

Pots

Earthy red, unglazed clay pots are preferred and are part of an honored tradition. These pots

are long lasting, are almost impossible to waterlog and are pleasant to handle.

Plastic pots are also available. They are lightweight, have drainage holes and require somewhat less watering than clay pots because the water does not evaporate through the sides of plastic. There are pre-seeded plastic pots available that come with their own plastic tray. All you have to do is to add water in order for the plants to germinate. Plastic pots in direct sunlight can heat up and cause plant damage.

Select the size pot that will comfortably accommodate the plant when it is full grown. Remember that a small seedling or a cutting will eventually be a large adult plant.

Small plants, for example, should live in small pots because there is less chance of the soil "souring" from overwatering.

Each pot should have a small saucer or pan beneath it to keep drainage water from running onto the floor or carpet. Some sand in the drainage container hastens evaporation of excess water.

Planters

Planters are large containers used to hold a number of plants. They can be made of pottery, wood, brass or plastic. Many homes come with built-in planters in front of large windows, as room dividers or elsewhere. Planters that are built in are usually made of stone, concrete or metal and are both rustproof and waterproof.

Metal containers should be coated with asphalt emulsions to prevent toxicity, as well as to prevent rusting and to keep the container waterproof.

A petcock at the bottom of the planter is helpful in draining out excess water.

A 3-inch layer of drainage materials such as pebbles or gravel is required at the bottom of the planter. Above that, a ½-inch layer of charcoal prevents stagnation of any standing water. The remainder of the planter is filled with sphagnum moss or peat moss to within 3 to 4 inches of the top.

Potting doubled potted plants in clay containers in planters is recommended. The clay per-

mits water movement into the pots quite readily. Plants with similar cultural requirements should be planted in a planter; check on available light when choosing specimens.

Pots make it easier to remove diseased plants and plants that outgrow the planter. If you use pots of different sizes you can place the smaller ones on inverted pots to make them all level. Fill in the spaces between pots with more peat.

Small planters can be set up with plants not already potted. Select plants that will grow at the same rate so that one will not shade another.

The following plants seem to be especially well adapted to planters. There are others you may wish to try.

African violet
Aucuba
Chinese evergreen
croton
dumb cane
maranta
philodendrons, small
pittosporum
pothos
screwpine
snake plant

Plants can be set directly into the planter, as well as being potted first.

In this planter the smaller pots are set on inverted pots to raise them to the same level as the larger pots.

Hanging baskets

Hanging baskets are best suited for areas of minimum traffic. It is disconcerting at the very best to bump your head on a clay pot, even if its resident is particularly attractive. The best spots are on a patio, in the kitchen over the sink near the window, along the screens of porches or on a balcony.

These are a problem however. Watering is a job, and if your kitchen is not well ventilated, rising warm air adds to the difficulties.

For indoors, use plastic pots to reduce moisture loss, and a plastic holder. For patio, porch or balcony, use a mesh or woven basket lined with damp moss into which the plants go. There are hanging baskets on the market with drainage holes.

Here is a partial list of basket plants you might use.

begonia
Christmas cactus
cissus
columnea, vine types
English ivy
ferns
fittonia
flame violet
fuchsia
German ivy
ivy geraniums
Kenilworth ivy
lantana
philodendron, vine types
pothos
shamrock
spider plant
strawberry geranium
string of hearts
velvet plant
wandering Jew
wax plant

Dish gardens

Dish gardens are creative and pure fun. Essentially, dish gardens are plantings of small, slow growing plants in open shallow dishes or containers.

Usually grown in dishes lacking drainage openings, watering is of major importance and over-watering a possibility. Always try to put ½-inch of charcoal, sand or gravel at the bottom to allow for drainage.

Carefully select plants with the same growth requirements for light and water.

After planting, spray the plants and soil until the soil is moist but not soaking. Then keep the dish in a shaded spot for about forty-eight hours,

Planters are available commercially that will put your window space to good use.

and move it into strong light for several days.

Watering is most efficient using a bulb sprayer

and is required four to seven times a week.

Dish gardens with only a single species of plant are attractive in their own right and are particularly nice in offices where care is sporadic and weekends long.

Cacti are much favored for dish gardens as are succulents. Other well-suited plants include:

This dish garden is occupied by a single plant.

African violet
aloe
bromeliads
Chinese evergreen
coleus
dracaena
dumb cane
English ivy, small varieties
evergreen seedlings
ferns, small, dwarf, and seedlings
fig
fittonia
geranium
kalanchoe
maranta
mosses
palm, miniature and dwarf
peperomia
philodendron, young
podocarpus
pothos
snake plant
strawberry geranium
wandering Jew
wax plant

A Plant Holder in Macramé

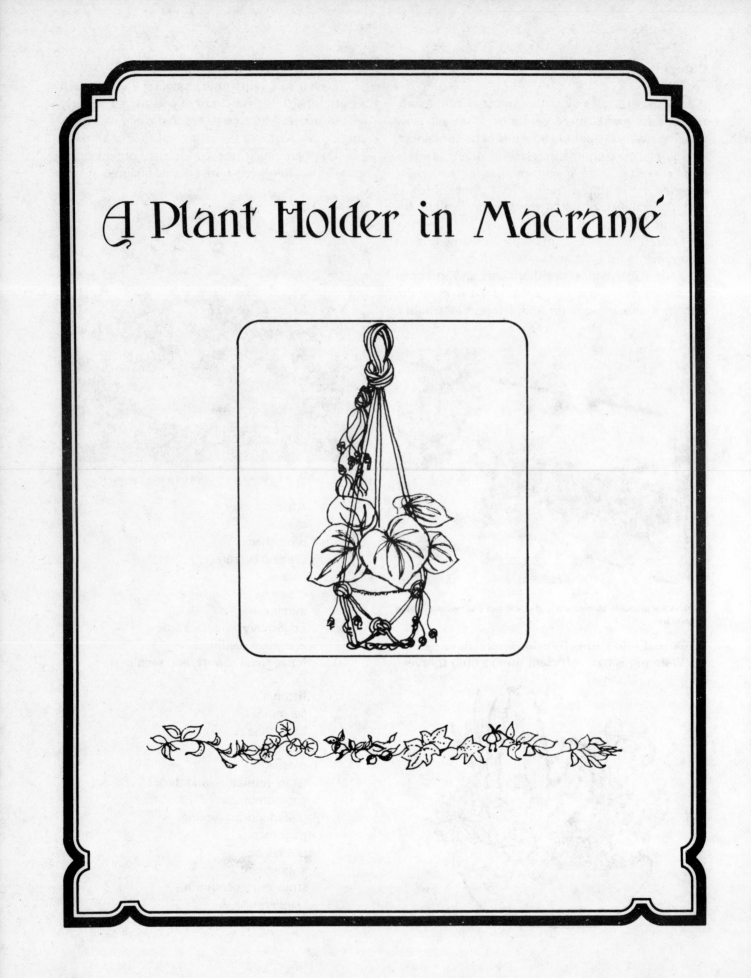

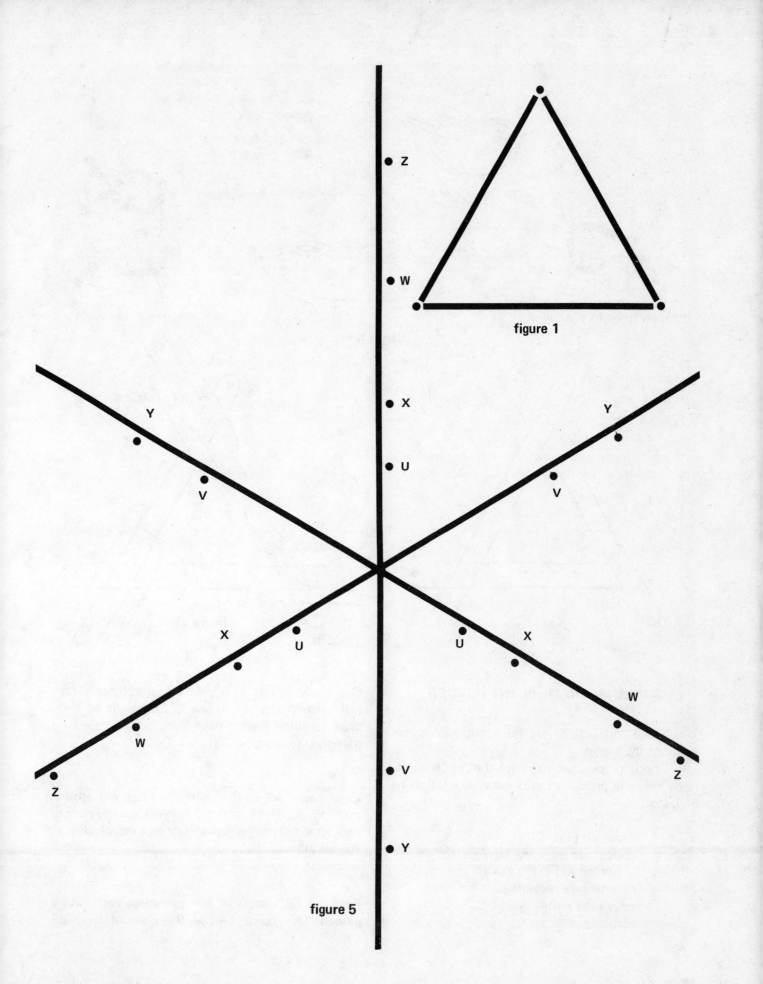

figure 1

figure 5

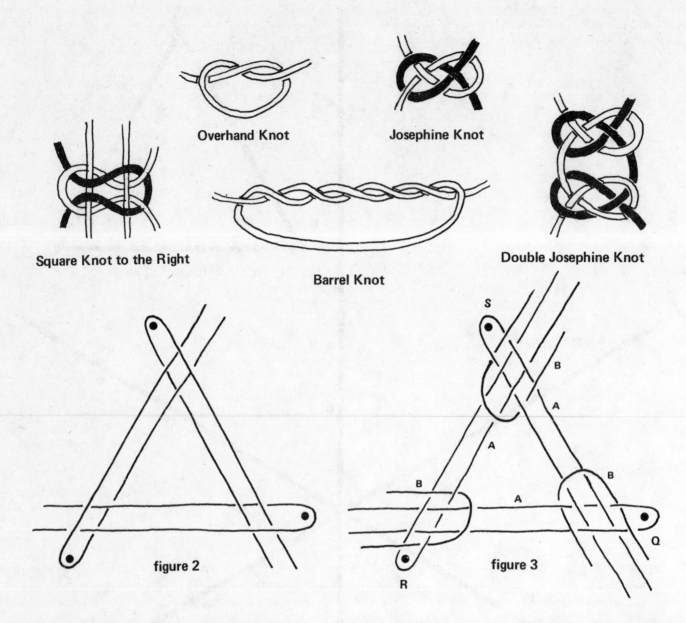

Overhand Knot

Josephine Knot

Square Knot to the Right

Barrel Knot

Double Josephine Knot

figure 2

figure 3

SMALL MACRAMÉ PLANT HOLDER

These instructions are for a pot with a diameter of 3½ inches.

Check to see that you have the proper materials. You will probably have most of the following on hand:

    T-shaped pins
    cork board or pillow (any surface on
        which to pin the work)
    ruler or tape measure
    scissors or knife
    cord

Cut three 9-foot ("A" cords) and three 5-foot ("B" cords) strands of cord. Tape ends to eliminate ravelling. Insert three pins in the shape of a triangle into the board. (figure 1)

Loop each "A" cord in half and place one around each pin (Q, R, S) in the triangle. Lace the ends of each strand through its neighboring loop, clockwise. (figure 2)

Fold the "B" cords in half and place each over a pinned "A" cord. Thread the ends of the "B" cords under the inner strands and over the outer strands of the "A" cords. (figure 3)

With the four strand ends on pin "Q" make a square knot to the right, with cord "B" over cord "A." (figure 4)

Repeat for cords "A" and "B" at pins "R" and "S." Pull all knots taut.

Trace or copy the pattern shown in figure 5. Remove the pins from your board and secure the pattern to the board. Repin the work at points "U," arranging each square knot against a pin.

Insert three pins at points "V" of the pattern. With two left strands of square knot from point "Q" (figure 4) and two right strands of the square knot from point "R" (figure 4) make a Josephine knot. Pull knot taut to pin at point "V."

Tie Josephine knots by using the two right strands from square knot at "Q" and the two left strands from square knot at "S." Repeat twice more, following figure 6 for the proper under-over sequence of the strands.

Insert three more pins at points "W." Tie another round of Josephine knots, again checking figure 6 for the proper sequence of the strands.

Insert strand 1 (figure 6) to the outside of the work by going through the center of the knot. Insert strand 2 (figure 6) to the inside of the work by going over and back through the center.

Repeat this last step with each Josephine knot, making sure the knots are evenly spaced.

Straighten out the remaining six strands. Then decide how long you want your plant holder to be. Next, make your loop, tying an overhand knot. Be sure to arrange the strands evenly. (figure 7)

To prevent strands from pulling through, tie another overhand knot in each of the three pairs of strands just below the loop.

Trim strands to three inches below the Josephine knots and four inches beyond the loop. You can then tie an overhand knot about one inch from the strand ends and fringe them. As an alternative, tie a barrel knot at the end of each strand. (figure 8)

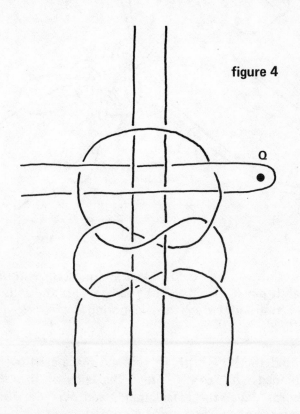

figure 4

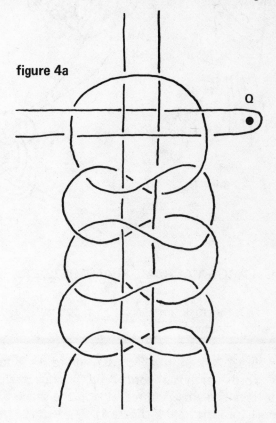

figure 4a

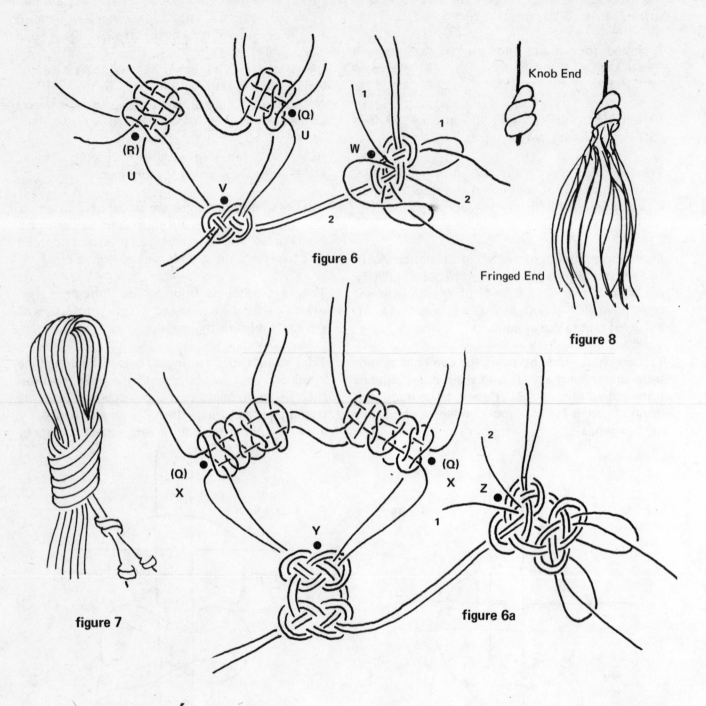

Knob End

figure 6

Fringed End

figure 8

figure 7

figure 6a

LARGE MACRAMÉ PLANT HOLDER

These instructions are for a pot with a diameter of 5 inches.

Cut three 12-foot ("A" cords) and three 8-foot ("B" cords) strands of cord. Tape the ends to eliminate ravelling. Insert three pins in the shape of a triangle into the board. (figure 1)

Loop each "A" cord in half and place one around each pin (Q, R, S) in the triangle. Lace the ends of each strand through its neighboring loop, clockwise. (figure 2)

Fold the "B" cords in half and place each over a pinned "A" cord. Thread the ends of the "B" cords under the inner strands and over the outer strands of the "A" cords. (figure 3)

With the four strand ends on pin "Q" make a square knot to the right, with cord "B" over cord "A." Immediately tie another square knot at that point. (figure 4a)

Repeat for cords "A" and "B" at pins "R" and "S." Pull all knots taut.

Trace or copy the pattern shown in figure 5. Remove the pins from your board and secure the pattern to the board. Repin the work at points "X," so that the last square knots rest against the pins.

Insert three pins at points "Y" of the pattern. With two left strands of square knot from point "Q" (figure 4) and two right strands of the square knot from point "R" (figure 4) make a Josephine knot. Pull knot taut to pin at point "Y." Repeat, tying a second Josephine knot right next to the first.

Repeat this process until you have a total of six Josephine knots in groups of twos. Follow figure 6a for the proper under-over sequence of the strands.

Insert three more pins at points "Z." Tie another round of double Josephine knots, again checking figure 6a for the proper sequence of strands.

Insert strands 1 and 2 (figure 6a) to the outside of the work by going through the center of the first knot.

Repeat this last step with each first Josephine knot, making sure the knots are evenly spaced.

Straighten out the remaining six strands. Then decide how long you want your plant holder to be. Next, make your loop, tying an overhand knot. Be sure to arrange the strands evenly. (figure 7)

To prevent strands from pulling through, tie another overhand knot in each of the three pairs of strands just below the loop.

Trim strands to four inches below the Josephine knots and five inches beyond the loop. You can then tie an overhand knot one-and-one-half inches from the strand ends and fringe them. As an alternative, tie a barrel knot at the end of each strand. (figure 8)

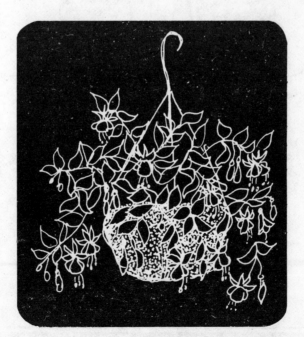

The Plants

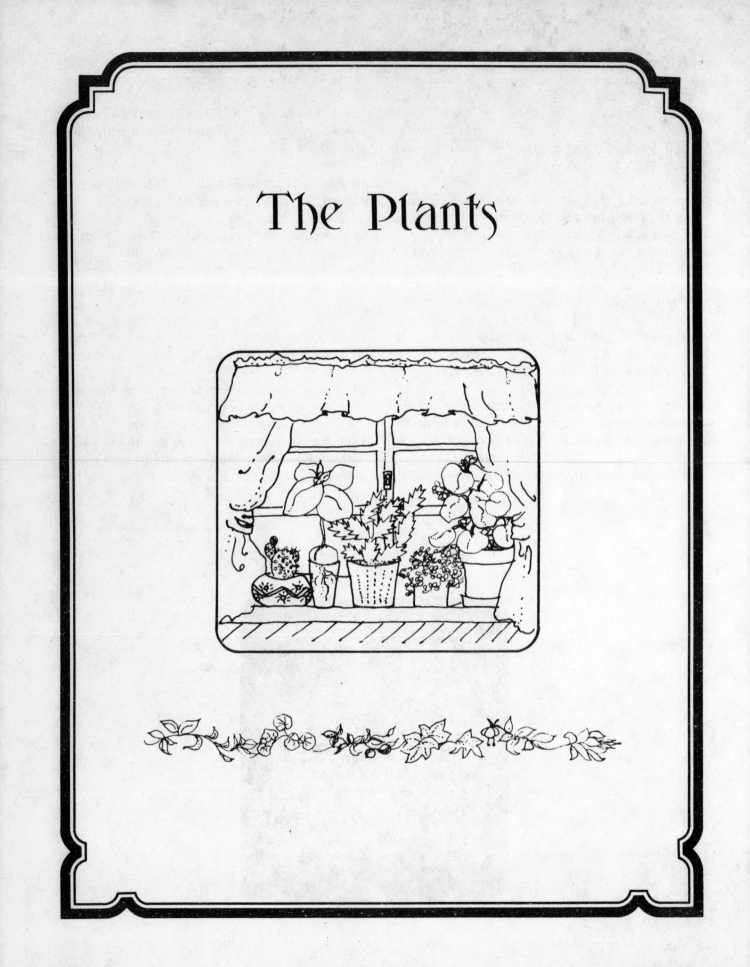

Saintpaulia ionantha

AFRICAN VIOLET

The African violet is perhaps the most popular of all house plants. Although a native of Kenya in Africa, most varieties will bloom a large part of the year in the home, if given indirect sunlight and a not-too-fertile soil that is well-drained and rich in humus. It will also grow very well under fluorescent lights. Water with moderate frequency, taking care not to let it dry out completely. A fairly constant temperature of between 65 and 70 degrees is required, both during the day and night. When in bloom, feed lightly every two to four weeks. Height: to about six inches. Colors: blossoms of blue, purple, white, and pink. It propagates fairly easily by leaf cuttings or separation of crowns.

ALOE

The aloe family is a large group of succulent plants from the Old World. Some varieties can grow to four feet tall. The leaves are usually narrow, up to a foot long and two-and-one-half inches wide. This native of tropical Africa does well in the dry air created by modern heating methods. It is evergreen and prefers a well-drained soil with some sand or fine gravel. Give it plenty of sun. Water moderately when in growth and when resting, just enough to keep it from shriveling. Propagate by seeds or offshoots which can be plucked or cut from the parent plant.

The sap of the "Aloe vera," and other varieties, may be used as a medicinal balm.

When young, the "Aloe zebrina" forms rosettes. When mature, it will annually produce tall clusters of red flowers.

Candelabra aloe can grow to fifteen feet when at home in a tropical garden.

Aloe vera →

← *Aloe zebrina*

↓ *Aloe arborescens*

34

Pilea cadieri

ALUMINUM PLANT

The aluminum plant is a rapid-growing, somewhat succulent plant. It has thin, although fleshy, opposite leaves that appear quilted and painted with silvery aluminum over the usual vivid green. It likes bright light, but not direct sunlight and will suffer from a lack of water if neglected. Grown primarily for the beauty of its leaves, the flowers are relatively inconspicuous. It is usually pinched back to keep it small and propagated by cuttings when it gets too leggy. A dwarf variety, Minima, with smaller leaves is slower growing and remains more compact. The aluminum plant is native to Vietnam.

AMARYLLIS

The plants usually found in cultivation are bulbous hybrids producing trumpet-shaped blooms up to eight inches across on stems which grow from one to two-and-one-half feet tall. Blooms early in spring under normal conditions. Plant bulbs using ordinary potting soil in pots slightly wider than the bulbs. Allow two-thirds of the bulb to protrude from the soil. Place in a sunny location and fertilize. Flowers come in a few weeks, the leaves usually appearing later. The blossom colors include red, salmon, rose, pink, white, and striped forms, mostly named as varieties.

ASPARAGUS FERN

Not a true fern, but a South African trailing or semi-climbing relative of the garden vegetable. The feathery foliage is ideal both as a hanging pot plant and as cut greenery in flower arrangements. With ordinary soil and care, it will survive for many years in the home. Prefers filtered sunlight. The soil should dry out between thorough waterings. It can be grown from seed, but propagation by division is the usual method.

↑ *Hippeastrum* ↓

← *Asparagus sprengeri*

Anthurium scherzerianum

ANTHURIUM

Along with its close relative, "A. andreanum," this plant of the American tropics will often grow and bloom indoors year after year. The flowers are inconspicuous and clustered on the pointed spadix. The colorful part is the long-lasting, waxy-looking spathe. For best results, add a little extra sand and humus to the potting soil. Give the anthurium good light, but not direct sun. It requires a fair amount of watering and an occasional feeding when active. Colors include white, pink, red, orange, and salmon.

Persea americana →

AVOCADO

Widely grown by devotees of the well-known tropical fruit, it starts readily from seed sown in a light soil. Or, if preferred, insert three toothpicks into the seed, fill a glass with water, and suspend the seed in the water by resting the toothpicks on the glass rim. Be sure to always place the rounded end of the seed down. No special soil, growing conditions or care is required. However, it makes a rather ungainly plant if not often pinched and pruned. If your specimen becomes too tall, discard and start another.

BABY'S TEARS

This tiny, creeping, almost moss-like plant originally comes from the islands of Corsica and Sardinia. Grown solely for its foliage, it makes an excellent ground, or soil, cover for larger pot plants, provided the moisture requirements are similar. It is also happy by itself in a terrarium or berry bowl. It cannot survive drying out of the soil or a parched atmosphere. Also, it must be shielded from direct, burning sunshine. Start new plants by division or cuttings of stems. Be on the lookout for snails and slugs.

← *Helxine soleiroli*

stitch-leaf begonia

rex begonia

iron cross begonia

merry christmas begonia

BEGONIA

Begonia

There are thousands of species and varieties of begonias. While in active growth, keep all begonias fairly well watered and fed. When growth ceases, reduce the watering and let them rest until growth starts again. They require good light, but not burning sun. As all begonias have the tendency to become leggy, pinch back and prune regularly to keep it bushy. Some varieties propagate readily from cuttings, others less so.

The begonia Rieger is a group of new, more or less tuberous, hybrids from Germany noted for their large flowers which are borne in great profusion. To date, the colors are confined to red and orange tones.

39

BANANA PLANT

This is a rather tall species of banana which can some-times reach a height of twenty feet, if conditions are favorable. In the Phillipine Islands it is often grown for the fiber in its leaf base. Where space permits, it does lend a tropical atmosphere, especially in atriums, plant rooms, greenhouses and around indoor swimming pools. It likes a loose soil, plenty of moisture, warmth, and light. For smaller areas, substitute the dwarf, or lady-finger, banana from southern China which grows to only about six feet and bears edible three-inch long fruit.

Musa textilis ⟶

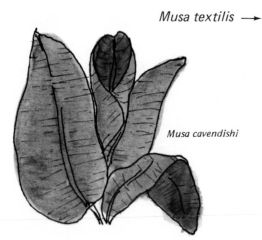

Musa cavendishi

BIRD'S-NEST FERN

An interesting and unusual fern of relatively easy culture from Asia (India to Japan). Its simple, undivided and un-cut leaves rise in rings leaving the center open. Under favorable conditions the fronds may reach a height of four feet and a width of eight inches. As a potted plant in the home, it rarely reaches such dimensions. Give it regular potting soil, good drainage, and an east or west window where it will receive indirect light only. Water thoroughly and mist daily; give it an occasional feeding. It is not readily propagated in the home; buy plants.

⟵ *Asplenium nidus*

BROMELIAD

Bromeliads are members of the pineapple family. Most are "air plants," growing on the bark and in the crotches of trees. The leaves of all bromeliads are stiff and decorated with various markings and colors. Keep them warm and moist, with water at all times in the cup formed at the center of the leaves. Although light is necessary to maintain the vividness of its markings, it prefers some shade. Propagate by offsets after flowering.

The striped urn plant is an attractive variety with broad leaves of blue-green, striped and variegated with cream at the margins.

The fingernail plant is so named for the rose-red color which tips its leaves.

Billbergia pyramidalis striata →

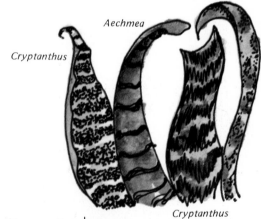

Cryptanthus   *Aechmea*   *Billbergia*

Cryptanthus

← *Neoregelias* ↓

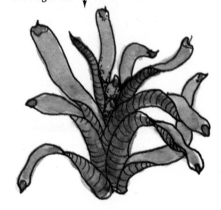

BROWALLIA

Actually a sub-shrub from tropical America, it is grown as an annual indoors in northern regions, and may be made to bloom at almost any season. Usually, it is grown in hanging baskets and induced to bloom in summer or winter. The star-like flowers may be blue, purple, or white. So far as possible, give it a cool location in good light. Permit the soil to dry between thorough waterings. Pinching back will encourage bushiness. In the home, it may be propagated by cuttings; commercially it is generally started from seed.

↑ *Browallia speciosa* →

BURRO'S TAIL

A most interesting succulent for hanging pots, the long stems of the burro's tail are clothed with spindle-shaped leaves that are short, thick, and bluish-green in color. As is characteristic of all succulents, the leaves are very fleshy. The modest pinkish flowers appear at the end of the stems. A native of Mexico, it needs only occasional watering and even less feeding, but it does require good light. It is ideal for use on porch and patio walls where it will thrive throughout the heat and drought of the summer season. A clipped stem will root readily in moist sand.

← *Sedum morganianum*

CACTUS

The cactus is a succulent native to the American tropics. It is characteristically fleshy with a thickened stem, and more often than not, exhibits spines. All cacti prefer some percentage of sand in their soil and good light. Also essential is good drainage. During growth, they require a fair amount of water; but be careful of overwatering. Water infrequently during rest periods. At home in the arid regions of the world, cacti also do well in apartments and homes where atmospheric humidity is low. The slow-growing cactus needs repotting only every two or three years. An occational misting will remove surface dirt from the plant when spines prevent cleaning by hand. Propagate by seed, cuttings, and offshoots.

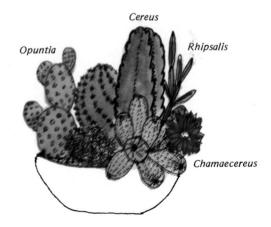

Opuntia

Cereus

Rhipsalis

Chamaecereus

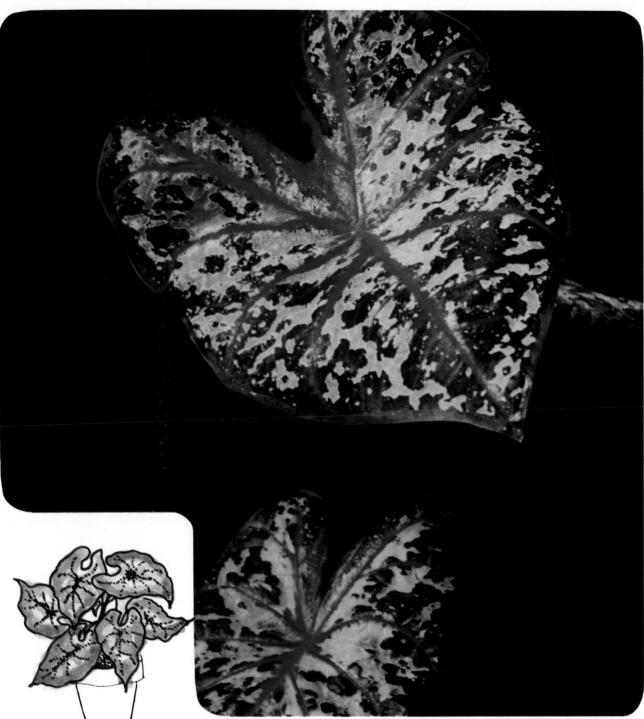

Caladium

CALADIUM

A most interesting group of hybrids grown from tubers for their colorful, fancy-patterned leaves. Coming from tropical America, they are draft-sensitive and do not take kindly to air conditioning. Grow them in fairly rich soil in a warm, well-lighted place, but out of direct sunshine. Water often enough to keep the soil slightly damp to the touch. In the fall cease watering and allow the foliage to die down. Rest three to four months in a warm place. Then water and start into growth again. Propagate by separating the tubers. Foliage colors include silver, white, green, pink, and red. In some plants the leaves may be veined with contrasting colors.

CALAMONDIN ORANGE

The calamondin orange is a citrus tree which can grow to eight or nine feet in height, under ideal conditions. In pots in the home, it will remain smaller, and as such makes an excellent indoor and patio evergreen. The small oranges are usually one to one-and-one-half inches in diameter and borne at the tips of the branches. The fruit is edible and may be used the same as lemons or limes. As with all citrus plants, give it good light. Ordinary soil and ordinary care complete the requirements. Reduce watering and feeding in winter. Native of China. Starts readily from seeds.

Citrus mitis →

CAMELLIA

Popular in the South as outdoor evergreen shrubs, they are grown indoors in the North in pots and tubs. However, they require a definitely cool place in winter, just safely above freezing. Give them a sandy, humusy soil made acid with peatmoss and, above all, do not plant deeply. Water and feed as necessary, especially during active growth, and keep from sudden changes in temperature. Many varieties exist that produce flowers in singles, doubles, and shades of pink, red, and white.

← *Camellia japonica* ↓

CHENILLE PLANT

Also known as the "red-hot cattail," this striking plant is a native of the East Indies. Outdoors, in favorable climates, it will grow as tall as fifteen feet; in pots, only to a manageable size. For best flowering, young and vigorous plants should be selected. Keep your plant warm and out of direct, burning sun. The soil should be kept evenly moist but not too wet; feed moderately. Propagated by cuttings with bottom heat, in late winter or spring. Subject to spider mites.

↓ *Acalypha hispida* →

CHINESE EVERGREEN

A native of Java, Borneo, and the Celebes Islands, the Chinese evergreen is one of the finest plants for indoor culture under conditions of poor light and neglect. It survives away from windows and in nothing but water. If grown in soil, allow the soil to dry between soakings. Because growth is slow, it seldom needs repotting or discarding because of size, making it ideal for small pots or containers on tables and shelves. The infrequent flowers are calla-like, two inches long and greenish white. Propagates readily by division or cuttings.

← *Aglaonema simplex*

Capsicum annuum

CHRISTMAS PEPPER

An attractive and small tropical plant of the potato family grown for its colorful peppers which appear only once, during the Holiday Season. Started from seed in March, they should be potted and grown without interruption for best results. They like warmth, even moisture and moderate feeding. Give it good light. Chills can check growth and cause leaf dropping. The flowers are small and white. The fruits of the variety Birdseye turn scarlet when ripe; Christmas Candle, waxy-yellow, then red. Both are edible, but rarely used so.

Coleus blumei

Coleus rehneltianus

Coleus blumei

COLEUS

Tender perennials grown primarily for their attractively colored and variegated foliage of green, yellow, red, and purplish in a myriad of patterns and combinations. Leaves may be ruffled, heart-shaped, oval or with tooth-like edges. Native to Java, it is easy to grow under ordinary conditions in the home or outdoors in summer. Good light encourages strong coloring. Can grow to three feet, but usually kept to about one foot by pinching to encourage bushiness. Young, vigorous plants started from cuttings at any time, or seeds in spring, make the best plants. When not pinched, small flowers of purplish-blue will appear.

CORAL BERRY

A handsome, small evergreen shrub from China and Japan sold primarily at Christmas. It carries its red berries all year—often as many as three years' crops at one time. Grow in good light but not burning sun. Give it ordinary care, regular potting soil and normal house temperatures. If attacked by scales, touch each culprit with a paint brush dipped in alcohol. The coral berry may grow as tall as three feet, but commonly grows to about one-and-one-half feet. Propagate from seeds or cuttings with bottom heat.

↓ *Ardisia crispa* →

CORN PLANT

Originally from tropical Africa, the corn plant is grown outdoors in the Deep South and in pots indoors in the North. They are undemanding plants and will grow under poor light conditions, but like warmth and constant moisture at the roots. Sudden chills or drafts may cause brown blotches or stop growth and bring on yellowish flowers. The variety shown is grown for its ornamental foliage which is a light green and yellow and up to 20 inches in length. Propagate by stem cuttings. If too tall, air-layer.

← *Dracaena* ↑

Columnea hybrida

COLUMNEA

"Goldfish plants" are mostly fibrous-rooted, tropical American plants frequently found growing on trees. Many in cultivation are vine-like or hanging to three feet. Leaves come in pairs; striking two-lipped flowers may be red, yellow, orange, or pink. Columneas grow best in a humid atmosphere and a fast-draining, porous soil mix. Water and mist frequently. They prefer to be kept warm and fed lightly but frequently when in active growth. Bud setting is encouraged in the winter by reducing water and temperature. Propagated by division, stem or tip cuttings.

Codiaeum variegatum pictum

CROTON

Shrubs from Malaysia, the south of India, etc. with attractive, thick alternate leaves. The leaves may be either plain or lobed; some are ribbon-like and curled. Leaf colors include brilliant greens, golds, and reds; the flowers are rather inconspicuous. Hence, the croton is grown chiefly for its exotic foliage. Give the croton any good soil, reasonable feeding, and warmth. It will survive in a shady spot in your home, but in order to develop the brilliant coloring, sun is absolutely vital. May be grown from seeds, but specific types must be propagated from cuttings of half-ripened wood over bottom heat. If they get too tall and leggy, shorten by air-layering the tops.

CROWN-OF-THORNS

A good plant for hot, dry homes and sunny windows. Native to Madagascar, it needs little care and stands rather desert-like conditions, although it may drop its leaves if allowed to get too dry. It grows up to four feet high, with very spiny angular stems. The small flowers, which normally appear around Easter, are a reddish-coral color and very attractive. Needs no special care. Propagated by stem cuttings. Attractive espaliered or flat as a pattern on a trellis.

← *Euphorbia splendens* →

DRACAENA

Another foliage plant that thrives in moderate to dim light. The upright stems of this variety bear neat, nine-inch, lance-shaped leaves with yellow and white stripes. Since the stems tend to be weak, it is better to have more than one plant in a pot. Its chief requirement is temperature—at least 65 degrees in winter. There are no unusual feeding and watering requirements. Native to the Congo region of Africa. Propagate by stem cuttings with bottom heat. If it gets too leggy, air-layer.

← *Dracaena sanderiana*

Clyclamen persicum

CYCLAMEN

A Near Eastern, autumn and winter-flowering plant with large, flat tubers and heart-shaped succulent, often interestingly marbled leaves. The flowers are large and butterfly-like; the colors ranging from white, to a vivid pink, to a deep red in single, double, and fringed forms. The soil should be well-drained but never allowed to dry out. For best results give moderately good light but keep as cool as possible when in bloom. High temperatures (over 65 degrees) can cause yellowing of the leaves and bud dropping. Too little light can have the same effect. Old bulbs can be rested and regrown, but new ones started from seeds 18 months before are better.

DUMBCANE

One of the group often referred to as dumbcanes because the leaves contain calcium oxylate. If the leaves are chewed, this chemical can cause temporary paralysis of the tongue, but is not otherwise harmful. Immediately rinsing with vinegar relieves this unpleasant symptom. The dumbcane is an excellent foliage plant for indoors. It withstands modern heat, dry air, poor light, and needs only moderate watering, although it will appreciate more sun and humidity if given. From Costa Rica, this dieffenbachia is a smallish plant with oblong, leathery, dark green leaves. Propagates rapidly by offsets or stem cuttings laid in moist sand.

Dieffenbachia
← *oerstedi* →

ENGLISH IVY

These evergreen shrubs from Europe, Asia and North Africa can climb 20 or more feet into trees by means of aerial rootlets, as well as function effectively as groundcovers. In their juvenile condition, they make fine small house plants. They survive all types of neglect, requiring ordinary potting soil and little sun. Permit the soil to dry completely between thorough waterings; an occasional misting is beneficial to the plant. In the home, they are often let trail from mantels and bookcases, but they make a more vigorous growth when trained upright on trellises. There are many varieties exhibiting differing leaf forms and variegations. Propagates readily from cuttings placed in ordinary soil.

← *Hedera helix* →

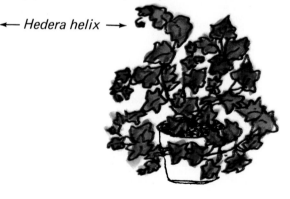

Echeveria

ECHEVERIA

Also known as hen-and-chickens. One of a large group of succulents, chiefly from Mexico, which grows in an attractive rosette form. Usually small and bluish gray-green, the rosettes appear even when the stems beneath have become elongated. It will annually produce flowers of orange, pink, or coral. Culture is the same as for other succulents and cacti. Give it a well-drained, sandy soil and plenty of sun. It requires as much water as other plants when in active growth, but only occasionally in winter when resting. It should also be kept cool at that time. If the plant appears shriveled, give more water. Feed lightly when in growth. Propagates by offsets, or "chicks," or more slowly from seeds or leaf cuttings.

Euphorbia lophogona

EUPHORBIA

One of a large group of more or less succulent trees, shrubs, and soft-stemmed plants characterized by a milky sap. This native of Madagascar is a shrub that generally grows to about two feet in height. It has four-angled, thorny branches and oblong leaves. The flowers come in clusters on stalks and have rounded bracts. Like cacti, it is undemanding in care and surroundings, but differs in its preference for warmth at night. Propagates from stem cuttings which have been allowed to heal a few days before insertion.

FALSE ARALIA

The false, or finger, aralia is a fast-growing, elegantly leaved plant of about 20 inches from New Caledonia in the Pacific. It has narrow, finger-like reddish-brown leaves with jagged edges and produces small, greenish flowers. It likes good, but not direct sunlight and some shade; an east window is ideal. Feed and water normally, although it does prefer humidity and will not thrive in very dry air. Prune frequently to maintain a compact form. Syringe forcefully with water to control mites. Starts from seed.

Dizygotheca elegantissima →

FIG

This native of tropical Africa is one of the lesser-known members of the large group of fig trees. A bushy tree, the thin branches are dense with rather long, leathery, dark green leaves that taper to a slender point. Unlike many figs, it fruits rather young, producing small, globular figs. Generally, figs like moderate to good light, fibrous loam and an even supply of moisture at root level. It does well indoors, even with air conditioning. Propagate by air-layering.

← *Ficus cyanthistipula*

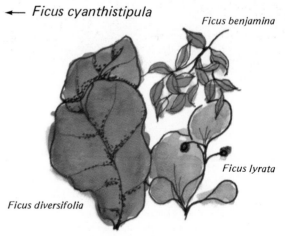

Ficus benjamina

Ficus lyrata

Ficus diversifolia

Fittonia verschaffelti argyroneura

FITTONIA

A small, ground-hugging plant with hairy, creeping stems. The flat, papery oval leaves of green netted with white veins (and sometimes red) make it an attractive foliage plant. A native of Peru, the fittonia prefers warmth, but beware of the warmth provided by modern heating methods as it tends to dry the air. High humidity is required. Consequently, it does best in the closed atmosphere of a terrarium or berry bowl. Give it good light with partial shade. The soil should be rich in humus, but well-drained; keep it moist, but not wet. Propagate by stem cuttings, taking care to include at least one joint.

Episcia punatata

FLAME VIOLET

One of the relatively new and not too widely known group of very attractive plants which are cousins of the popular African violet. All are low-growing, fibrous-rooted plants that creep along, rooting at the joints or cascading over their pots. Place it in an east window. It needs a temperature range of not less than 60 degrees when growing and 50 degrees in winter. Preferring warmer temperatures, leaves may darken or the plant may go dormant if kept too cool. Protect it from drafts. High humidity is a must, so mist daily. The flowers are a vibrant red-orange, hence the name flame violet. Native to Guatemala and Mexico. Propagate by offsets.

Fuschia hybrida

FUSCHIA

One of the many hybrids based upon species originating from the area ranging from Mexico to the tip of South America. It is an ideal hanging basket plant, the flowers in shades of pink, red, rose, fuschia, and blue forming a colorful cascade. They like a soil rich in garden loam and a window with good light, but will not survive in an atmosphere that is too warm or dry. Feed and water well while active for good flowering. Prune to keep it from getting too gangly. Reduce watering in September to bring on the rest period. It may be kept over winter if placed in a relatively dry cold cellar or frost-free garage. Or, they may be started anew each spring from cuttings of such plants.

GARDENIA

This is the gardenia widely sold for house plants: an everlasting double-flowered form of the Chinese Cape jasmine. It is an evergreen shrub with glossy leaves and strongly fragrant white blossoms. Give it good light, 65 degrees at night (58 degrees in December), a moist atmosphere, an acid, peat-filled soil that drains well, and a moderate but steady supply of moisture. Bud drop is caused by drafts and drought. Started in winter and summer from cuttings with three or four buds. Place in sand with bottom heat.

↓ *Gardenia jasminoides* →

GRAPE IVY

From the West Indies and South America, a moderate-growing very adaptable vine. It has brown, hairy stems, grape-like tendrils, and three-parted shiny green leaves. It makes a neat, not-too-rampant house plant with no special cultural needs. Give it ordinary soil, regular household conditions, ordinary feeding and watering. Not even good light is absolutely necessary. If it gets too leggy, nip it back. It can be put out in the summer. Propagates readily from stem cuttings and separation of roots.

← *Cissus rhombifolia*

Pelargonium hortorum

GERANIUM

This is the common geranium of the florist, but not the botanist. It is a hybrid form based upon species apparently originating in South Africa. It loves full sunshine, not too rich a soil, and only moderate watering. Prune frequently to keep it shapely and pluck dying blossoms to encourage new ones. It must be pot-bound or it will not flower! Colors: blossoms of red, white, pink, and salmon to orange. Starts readily from seed or cuttings allowed to heal for several days before plunging into sand. In winter, keep it cool and give good light. Other forms include: Martha Washington, scented, ivy and miniature geraniums.

GERANIUM IVY

Pelargonium peltatum

Related to the common geranium of the florist, it is trailing by nature with ivy-shaped leaves in shades of shiny green which may be variegated with cream and pink. A strong bloomer, the flowers and foliage make an impressive display that cascades from window boxes and hanging baskets. Good light and the average temperature (but cool in winter) and humidity ranges found in the home keep it healthy. As with the common variety of geranium, flowering is encouraged when somewhat pot-bound. Allow the soil to approach dryness between thorough waterings. Feed when in flower; cease during its rest periods. Propagate by cuttings, spring or fall.

Sinningia speciosa

GLOXINIA

A most attractive tuberous plant with relatively short stems, large velvety leaves and huge bell-shaped flowers. In some varieties, the flowers may be ruffled or frilled. Blossom colors include white, red, red with white edges, purple, blue, and violet and blue combined. Plant the tubers in February or March, covering them with one inch of soil. Flowering usually occurs from May to October. Give it a well-drained, peaty soil, no direct sunshine (east or west window), a moderate but steady supply of moisture and moderate feeding. When flowering ceases, dry off and store at 45 degrees until the next year. Propagate by seeds, leaf or stem cuttings.

HOLLY FERN

One of the best ferns for indoor use, the holly fern is noted for being tough and durable. A first choice for city-dwellers, it will thrive in a hotter and drier climate than other ferns. A native of China, India, Japan and Hawaii, it has thick, shining, leathery fronds rising on brown scaly stems from the short rhizomes. Variety Rochfordianum is even more robust and compact. All it takes is a reasonable soil, reasonable watering, an occasional feeding, and not too hot a location. An excellent table fern. Propagates by division.

Cyrtomium falcatum rochefordianum ⟶

HONDURAS RUBBER PLANT

The original species comes from the tropical rain forests of India and Malaya. It is an attractive fool-proof and excellent plant for the house. It has no special requirements, except that it be fed and watered occasionally and kept out of the burning sunshine. Wash the leaves every few weeks to keep them clean and shining. Pinch, if needed, to induce branching and air-layer when it gets too tall. Although it is rarely practiced in the home, it is possible to propagate from cuttings.

⟵ *Ficus elastica* ↓

Solanum pseudo-capsicum

JERUSALEM CHERRY

Frequently grown as a pot plant for use at Christmas time, it is an obliging and relatively easy, as well as attractive, little plant. It rarely grows more than 12 inches tall and produces dark green leaves and globular, orange-scarlet fruits. However, don't be tempted to taste the fruit, as it is poisonous. The summer flowers are white, but not terribly conspicuous. Give it partial, to full sun. Mist frequently (it likes humidity) and coolish temperatures. Native to Madeira. Because it is an annual, discard when it begins to tire and start new plants from seeds for the next year.

Kalanchoe

KALANCHOE

There are many kinds of kalanchoe and a number of these are commonly available from plant shops. Most of these winter-blooming succulents originated in Madagascar. The leaves are characteristically fleshy, some with a hair-like covering or scalloped edges. It prefers good light and average to cool room temperatures. The humidity range found in the home suits its needs and it should be watered when the surface of the soil is dry to the touch. Propagation is very easy to accomplish by planting seeds, taking leaf or stem cuttings, or division. Some types produce plantlets at their leaf edges, complete with aerial roots. Simply place these on moist soil to encourage their development.

Cissus antarctica →

KANGAROO VINE

As its name might suggest, the kangaroo vine hails from Australia. A close relative of the grape ivy, it too, makes a good, easy-to-care-for house plant that tolerates the warm and dry or air conditioned atmosphere of modern dwellings. Give it good but not burning sunlight and ordinary potting soil. Allow the soil to dry between thorough waterings. Feed moderately while in growth, eliminating the food during its rest period. A good plant for all exposures, but not south windows. Grow from cuttings.

JADE PLANT

An attractive South African plant also known as the money tree and the Chinese rubber plant. It is a freely-branching sturdy succulent with an enormously stout trunk and branches. The leaves are also thick. While it can eventually grow to nine feet, it is rarely seen over two feet tall. It is very tolerant of neglect and, while it likes sun, it will survive in dark hallways and rooms. It is also impervious to drafts and air conditioning. Plant it in potting soil with sand and a little humus added. The soil should dry for several days before rewatering. Cuttings root very readily, even in a glass of water.

← *Crassula argentea*

Aeschynanthus splendidus

LIPSTICK PLANT

Of Asiatic origin, this type is a man-made hybrid. It is a robust trailer with tapering leaves and erect, curving tubular flowers of orange-red blotched with maroon-red coming in large clusters. Normally growing on trees, they need excellent drainage when potted, as well as high humidity and frequent watering, except in winter. Flowers in spring; cut back the tendrils after the blossoms fade. Propagated by stem cuttings.

MAIDENHAIR FERN

Long a greenhouse favorite but not as happy in modern homes unless they can be provided with sufficient moisture in the air and assured that the soil ball will never dry completely. Nevertheless, it is well worth trying to culture this fragile beauty because of its slender, graceful black stems and vivid green foliage. Keep it out of the sunlight and away from heat sources, although it does like warmth. If happy, the crown may be readily divided. A native of Brazil.

Adiantum raddianum ⟶

MOTHER FERN

From the rain forests of Australia, New Zealand and Malaya comes this interesting fern. While its feathery fronds look much like many other indoor and outdoor ferns, it is different in one aspect: tiny plants grow on top of the fronds. These may be readily detached and potted to grow as new plants, if kept from drying. Give it good drainage and keep it reasonably moist. It likes to be kept warm, but out of direct sun. As with all ferns, high humidity is required, so mist often. Feed lightly when growing.

⟵ *Aspenium bulbiferum*

70

MYRTLE

Aromatic, subtropical shrubs frequently grown as a single trunk-like small tree in tubs. When rubbed, the glossy evergreen leaves have a spicy scent and the small, white flowers are sweet-smelling. Often put outdoors for the summer, especially in Europe. Permit the soil to dry between thorough waterings. They like a cool, well-lighted place and careful watering in winter. Propagation is usually by cuttings of half-ripened wood in summer. At home in Greece and neighboring regions.

Myrtus communis →

NORFOLK ISLAND PINE

Also known as starpine and Christmas tree plant, it is used for just that purpose in warm places. In its natural habitat in the South Pacific it makes a giant evergreen 120 feet tall. Indoors it is either discarded when too tall or the top is air-layered into a new plant. Under no circumstances should the lead shoot be lost. Otherwise, it is tolerant of nearly everything: hot sun, shade, drafts, heat, occasional drying. Side shoots will not make upright plants. Grow from seed.

← *Araucaria excelsa*

Rhoeo spathacea

MOSES-IN-THE-CRADLE

This plant from Mexico and the West Indies is grown in the open in Florida, but also does well in the home. The leaves are 12 inches long and three inches wide; dark green above and purple beneath. The plant, which makes an erect-spreading clump, is quite attractive. The small white flowers are nearly concealed. Does best out of direct sun. Likes warmth and humidity. Feed and water reasonably during growth, give less water and no food in winter. Propagate by side shoots in spring.

Nerium oleander

OLEANDER

Evergreen shrubs with slender, willowy stems growing to six, eight feet and more, if permitted. Coming from southern Europe and North Africa, it likes sunny, hot, dry places. The clusters of white, pink and red flowers are sometimes touched with yellow and grow on wood of the current year. So, plants can be pruned as needed just before new growth starts in spring. Water well when flowering. An ideal tub plant. All parts are poisonous if eaten. Cuttings root easily in water.

Nephrolepis exaltata →

NORWOOD FERN

This is a much-cut, lacey variety of the Boston fern which, in turn, is a variety of the sword fern found from Florida to Brazil, southern Asia and Australia. Like Whitmani, it is short, broad, fresh green and dense with wiry brown stems. It likes good light, but not burning sun, and moderate coolness. It tolerates air conditioning but not drafts and likes moist air. Like the others, it throws out threadlike runners from which new plants grow.

PALM

Also known as the "parlor palm," this is a dwarf, mountain palm from southern Mexico. It is even more dwarfed and slow growing than its parent species. Today, it is the most common indoor palm. Excellent in shady places, it stands all kinds of abuse and neglect, including air conditioning, which makes it an ideal plant for use in offices. Feed and water as conditions dictate in order to keep it evenly moist. Give it potting soil with equal parts of loam, sand and peat moss added. Grow from seed started in peat moss that is kept warm and moist.

← *Chamaedorea elegans bella*

The figure shows orchids labeled: Paphiopedilum, Oncidium, Cattleya, Cycnoches

ORCHID

Cattleya

There are thousands of orchid species, varieties, hybrids and multiple hybrids, many more or less similar. We shall not try to distinguish between them. All members of this group produce showy flowers of white, rosy tones, purple or yellow. They are usually grown in pots of fir bark, fern root, or shredded tree fern where they can get good circulation of warm moist air. Give good light without burning sun and water through at least once a week. Feed occasionally. Divide if too thick.

Oxalis

OXALIS

Often referred to as shamrock, lucky clover, or good-luck plant, it is a member of the herbaceous wood sorrel family. There are over 300 widely distributed species and 20 or more sorts in cultivation. The leaves are delicate and clover-like; the simply-shaped flowers bloom in tones of rose, yellow, and white. Most are easy to grow in pots as hanging basket plants; some varieties remain more compact. Give it a sunny, airy window. Feed moderately and water with enough frequency to keep the soil evenly moist. Most varieties rest in winter by ceasing to grow or dying down; be sure to reduce watering at this time. Propagate by divisions of the roots or bulbs.

Philodendron oxycardium →

PHILODENDRON

This is the most common and widely grown of all philodendron and it is practically fool-proof to cultivate. From the New World regions of Puerto Rico, Jamaica, and Central America, it is a small, vining plant with thick, heart-shaped leaves. Although it will grow as a hanging plant, it does better if allowed to grow upward on a trellis. It will stand more abuse than almost any house plant: poor light, lack of water, cold drafts, etc. Ideally, it does prefer warmth and reasonably good light. Easily propagated from cuttings.

PHILODENDRON

The "panda" philodendron is also known as the "fiddle-leaf" or "horsehead" philodendron. It is a much larger, bolder and more vigorous plant than the common philodendron, but it does not tolerate poor light and neglect as well. It has olive green, rather irregularly shaped leaves. A handsome climber, it is not grown as a hanging plant. Native of southern Brazil and propagated by stem cuttings or by air-layering when too large.

← *Philodendron panduraeforme*

watermelon-begonia

variegated

emerald ripple

Peperomia verschaffelti

PEPEROMIA

From the region of the upper Amazon comes this small succulent member of the pepper family often referred to as the "sweetheart peperomia." It makes a small, compact, short-stemmed rosette of more or less heart-shaped leaves. The surface is waxy and bluish-green with silver bands between the sunken veins. Give it the moderate light of an east or west window and good drainage. Water when the soil just begins to feel dry, but do not over water as this will cause stem rot. Propagate by division of crowns and by cuttings in rooting medium.

PIGGYBACK PLANT

Also called the "pick-a-back" plant, it is a truly native American plant from the moist woodland areas extending from California to Alaska. Its fuzzy, light green foliage grows in an open rosette form. Not particularly glamorous, it is grown primarily as a conversation piece, as it has the curious ability to produce small plants at the base of its mature leaf blades. To grow these, cut them off and place them in moist sand or water. It requires only ordinary care, tolerating poor light, but the soil must not be allowed to dry out completely.

Tolmiea menziesi ⟶

⟵ *Pittosporum tobira*

PITTOSPORUM

An evergreen shrub from China and Japan with attractive leathery leaves. A variegated form has leaves margined with cream. Widely grown outdoors in the South, it makes a good tub plant in the North where it stays a manageable size for years. The flowers are small, creamy, clustered at the branch tips and orange-blossom scented. Stands sun or shade, coolness or warmth, drafts and air conditioning. Give it ordinary soil. Water and feed moderately in growth, give it less water later. Mist foliage. Grow from seeds or half-ripened cuttings. Adaptable to bonsai.

Euphorbia pulcherrima

POINSETTIA

Unquestionably, the best known Christmas plant is this shrub from Mexico. Until recently, it was fragile for growing in the North, losing its leaves and colorful bracts with a draft. Now, some varieties have been developed that will hold them until summer. White, pink and multi-hued varieties are available in addition to the popular red. Give good light, keep warm and water as soil begins to dry. Beginning late September, put it into dark daily for four to six weeks (to reduce length of day to less than 12 hours) to initiate bloom which comes 10 to 12 weeks later. Start from cuttings in early summer.

PONY-TAIL PLANT

Also called bottle palm, it is a tree-like plant with an upright trunk swollen and balloon-like at the base. Its long, narrow leaves hang down in mop-like fashion. The flowers are small, clustered, and whitish. Like some desert plants, it can store a whole year's supply of water. Native to Mexico. Indoors, give it sun and warmth in summer. A slow grower, it needs little food and rare watering, but after many years it may attain a height of 30 feet. In winter, keep it cooler and do not water. Grow from seeds or remove offsets.

Beaucarnea recurvata →

← *Scindapsus aureus*

POTHOS

Also known as "devil's-ivy." Coming from the monsoon area of Malaysia, it is a tall-growing climber with large, waxy green leaves variegated with creamy-yellow. In the juvenile state it makes an excellent small pot plant or subject for hanging containers or water culture. It can take extreme heat and poor light, but it should be kept fairly dry at the roots. Feed gently to keep it small. The flowers are calla-like. The Marble Queen is the most common variety. Propagate by tip or joint cuttings.

PRAYER PLANT

A Brazilian first cousin to arrowroot, the prayer plant is grown for its foliage. It is low-growing, reaching only about a foot and the leaves which hug the ground fold upward in the evening as if in prayer. They are grayish-green with a row of chocolate or dark green blotches on either side. The small flowers are white with purple stripes. Give it moderate light, warmth, and constant moisture, except from December to February when it rests. Divide when growth begins.

*Maranta leuconeura
κerchoveana* ⟶

RABBIT'S-FOOT FERN

One of the most interesting, graceful and easily-grown ferns, it is characterized by finely-cut foliage rising from rhizomes covered with brown hairs like a rabbit's foot. Since it grows on trees, it needs water only occasionally, even when grown in hanging baskets of chopped sphagnum and fern root or chopped tree fern. Mist frequently. Feed lightly and only occasionally. Prefers part shade. The rhizomes can be divided to make new plants. Native to the Fiji Islands.

⟵ *Davallia fejeensis* ↓

RHOEO

A perennial herb from Mexico and the West Indies. The leaves are a foot long, three inches wide and of dark green striped with pale yellow above and purple beneath. The small, white flowers are partly concealed. It differs from its relative, Moses-in-the-cradle, only by its striped leaves. A very tolerant plant, it will grow even when conditions are not ideal. Give it moderate light and the temperature and humidity range of the average house. Propagates readily from seeds and offsets.

Rhoeo spathacea vittata ⟶

SELAGINELLA

A moss-like, branching, flowerless, little plant which hugs the soil making an ideal groundcover for large tubs, planter areas and conservatory soils. Very easy to grow in shaded, moist places or large terrariums. While it likes warmth, it is not absolutely necessary. It propagates readily from cuttings covered lightly with moist sand and placed in a flat covered with plastic. There are dwarf, yellowish, and variegated types as well.

⟵ *Selaginella kraussiana*

83

SILVER-LACE FERN

This is a variegated table fern which is a small and highly satisfactory subject for indoor culture. It has slightly leathery fronds with a broad band of creamy-white down the center of each leaflet. The stalks are graceful and wiry. Not only is it good as a table subject but also as a covering for the leggy stems of other plants. Ideal for culture in terrariums. It is not at all particular about growing conditions or care. The rhizomes can be divided when large enough. From tropical and sub-tropical regions.

Pteris cretica albo-lineata →

SNAKE PLANT

A fool-proof plant that can survive through the worst neglect: poor light, no water, heat, dry air, cold drafts, etc. It makes a vase-like rosette of broadly elliptical leaves cross-banded with gray, cream, and green with golden yellow bands alongside of the margins. Water occasionally and feed even less. It may flower if pot-bound, but generally it is grown for its persistent foliage. Propagated from offshoots or leaves which have been cut horizontally into sections and plunged upright into wet sand. South African in origin.

← *Sansevieria trifasciata* ↓

84

Beloperone guttata

SHRIMP PLANT

An everblooming, generally shrub-like plant from Mexico which reaches a maximum height of about 30 inches. The curious flowers attract all of the attention. The true flowers are small but peak out from beneath reddish-brown bracts which are arranged in drooping, hop-like clusters that are reminiscent of cooked shrimps. Flowers from fall through spring. It has no special requirements. Give it good light and warmth. Water when the surface of the soil becomes dry. Prune frequently. Feed moderately while active. It can be grown from cuttings taken at any time. Other varieties produce bracts of bright green or bright red.

SEA GRAPE

Native to the southern coastal regions of Florida and south, it makes a tree up to 20 feet and a good tub or house plant for large areas or patios in summer. Its leaves are round, up to six or eight inches across, leathery and shiny. The fragrant flowers are white and come in clusters 10 inches long. The fruits, which are grape-like and purple, can be used for jelly. Prefers good light and reasonable warmth. Keep the soil evenly moist. Start from seed or propagate by air-layering.

Coccoloba uvifera →

SOUTHERN YEW

From China and Japan, it grows outdoors in our South but makes a good, narrow evergreen with slender leaves for indoor use in tubs in the North. It shears well and can be shaped as desired. While not overly conspicuous, the female tree bears berry-like purplish fruits. Although preferring sun, it can survive with moderate light. Keep soil moist but well-drained. Feed moderately during growth but permit rest. Grows from seeds and cuttings. Adaptable to bonsai.

← *Podocarpus macrophyllus maki* ↓

86

SPATHIPHYLLUM

The "Cleveland spathiphyllum" is an improved variety and, perhaps, the most widely-known. The thin, leathery leaves are lance-shaped and long-stemmed. The flowers are white and calla-like. Rarely growing over 18 inches in height, it is a convenient size for most homes. Also, it tolerates moderate to poor light conditions. It will take room temperatures and dryness in its stride. Feed it occasionally and keep the soil evenly moist. Propagation is readily accomplished by division, usually in the spring and early summer.

↓ *Spathiphyllum clevelandi* →

SPIDER PLANT

From South Africa and a good hanging basket plant for beginning gardeners. It grows readily under almost any condition. The long and narrow leaves arch gracefully while long stalks appear from the heart and bear the small white flowers, followed by tufts of leaves with aerial roots. Propagation is easily accomplished by planting these offspring or by dividing the parent plant with its fleshy roots. Give them ordinary feeding, watering, heat and light conditions. Variety Variegatum is attractively white-striped.

← *Chlorophytum comosum*

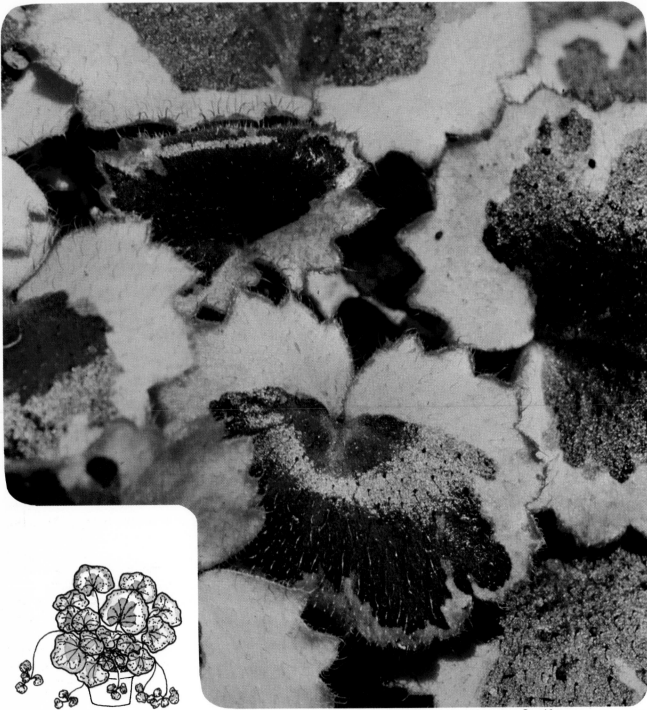

Saxifraga sarmentosa

STRAWBERRY GERANIUM

Also called "strawberry begonia," it is a small but interesting plant from China and Japan, suitable for covering the ground or growing in hanging baskets. The leaves are round, reddish below and spattered with white veins above. Most interesting are the long, wiry stolons from which tiny plants spring. Its culture is easy, but it does best in good light and not too much heat. Although it should be kept evenly moist, allow the soil to approach dryness occasionally. Propagate by potting these plantlets. The variety Tricolor is multi-colored.

STAGHORN FERN

The fertile fronds of the triangle staghorn are twice-forked. As with all species, the sterile fronds are flat discs which clasp the tree or other support upon which it grows. In time, these dry and take on a parchment-like appearance. Grow on slabs of wood to which a ball of sphagnum moss is wired, in wire baskets, or on slabs of tree fern. Drench occasionally, either by dipping into or pouring on water. Add dilute fertilizer from time to time. Propagate from offshoots. West African in origin.

Platycerium stemaria ⟶

STREPTOCARPUS

The "Cape primrose" comes originally from South Africa. The leaves are long, lance-shaped and yellow-green in color. It is a prodigious bloomer. The tubular flowers come in clusters and may be blue, violet, or white. Give it good light and high humidity. Keep the roots evenly moist at all times. Feed often while in active growth. Propagate by planting seeds in winter, or, as with hybrids, by dividing the clumps.

⟵ *Streptocarpus*

STRING OF HEARTS

A wiry vine from South Africa, it has small, fleshy oval green leaves in pairs along a thinly-clothed, thickish stem. The odd, lantern-like flowers are green with purplish markings on the outside and purplish-black inside. It makes an ideal conversation piece. Being somewhat succulent, it is easy to care for. Keep reasonably moist in summer, drier in winter, but always in well-drained soil. It requires moderate light conditions and the temperature range of the average house. Propagate by division, stem cuttings, or by planting the bulblets which develop along the stems.

Ceropegia caffrorum →

SWEDISH IVY

Another ideal plant for beginners that can sucessfully withstand even the worst of care. The thick, round leaves with scalloped edges clothe weak stems. An attractive hanging plant for pots, baskets and wall containers. Give it ordinary soil, passable light, occasional water, a little fertilizer now and then. Propagation, too, is easy. Just pinch off some stem pieces and place in either water or soil.

← *Plectranthus australis* ↓

SWEET OLIVE

A fragrant shrubby relative of the true olive, it makes an excellent house and patio plant. A slow-growing evergreen, it has glossy holly-like leaves and is distinguished from that group by its opposite leaves. The flowers are small, whitish and with the fragrance of jasmine. Give it a good, well-drained soil, good light and keep it cool and slightly moist. From the Himalayas, China and southern Japan. Propagate from cuttings using a rooting hormone in moist sand and peat.

↓ *Osmanthus fragrans* →

SWISS CHEESE PLANT

A large plant from southern Mexico and Guatemala, it is ideal for growing against a slab of wood in a dark corner away from light sources. It needs minimum care and easily adapts to conditions found in modern homes. If the plant ceases to produce split and holed leaves, it needs envigorating, either with more fertilizer, better light, or both. Sponge the leaves frequently to keep them clean and shining. It may be propagated by cuttings, air-layered, or planted from seed.

← *Monstera deliciosa* ↓

Gynura aurantiaca

VELVET PLANT

Also known as "purple passion" or "purple velvet" plant, this is another plant grown almost exclusively for its foliage, although it does produce orange disc-like flowers. It is non-woody, with stout stems and broad, toothed green leaves that are covered with purple fuzz and veined with a deeper purple. Give it a not-too-rich soil, plenty of sun to encourage vivid coloring, and moderate amounts of water. As it has the tendency to become leggy, prune frequently. It is readily grown from cuttings of growing shoots and from seeds, if obtainable. A native of Java.

UMBRELLA TREE

In its native habitat in New Zealand, this makes a small tree of 20 to 25 feet. Indoors, it has become common wherever large plants are used and will remain a manageable size. The leaves "umbrella" into the form of a seven-to-ten-fingered hand. Grow it in a large pot or tub of ordinary soil. Water, permit the soil to dry and rewater. It does not like excessive heat or drought. It can be grown from seed, but they are not readily available. Propagate by cuttings of half-ripened stems.

Schefflera digitata →

VENUS FLYTRAP

A unique and interesting plant that rarely grows over a few inches tall. Native to the southeastern United States, it grows from tiny bulbs. Although it does produce white flowers, of principal interest are the leaves which snap together when triggered by the touch of an insect. The captives are then digested to supply missing nutrients. Grow in constantly moist acid peat moss and sand in an open container or terrarium. Keep cool in winter to permit rest. Propagate by seeds, bulblets, division, or leaf cuttings.

← *Dionaea muscipula*

93

VICTORIA FERN

Also known as the "silver table fern" and a close relative of the silver-lace fern, it is an ideal small subject for use on tables and other places away from windows. The leaflets are banded with white bordered by wavy margins of rich green. Particularly suited to dish gardens and terrariums. Its care and propagation are similar to the silver-lace fern. Its parent species is native of the region extending from the Himalayas to Ceylon, Queensland (Australia), and Samoa.

Pteris ensiformis →

WAX PLANT

The miniature wax plant is a dwarf with branches that stand upright at first and then droop. It is not a climber. The thick, waxy oval leaves are deep green with a brown band along the midrib. The unusual, long-lasting waxy flowers are white with purple centers. Tolerant of heat and some drought, but they do prefer consistent care. The flowers grow from spurs . . . do not cut them off! Turning plants sometimes hinders flowering. Propagate by cuttings. Originally from India.

← *Hoya bella*

94

Zebrina pendula

WANDERING JEW

Long a very popular and common house plant, it is ideally suited for use as an indoor groundcover, hanging basket plant, or simply cascading over its pot. The leaves are deep green to purple with two broad, silvery bands and a vivid purple beneath. It is highly tolerant, growing where it is cool or warm, light or shaded. It is somewhat succulent and therefore tolerant of lapses in watering. Propagates readily from cuttings placed in water. Originally from Mexico.

Aphelandra squarrosa

ZEBRA PLANT

A Brazilian import and a striking plant when in bloom. It is robust, with stiff, reddish stems and glossy dark green leaves contrastingly veined with white. The small, pale yellow flowers are inconspicuous, but housed in showy, upright spikes of orange-yellow bracts which are very long-lasting. Flowers best, summer or fall, if not pot-bound. Give good light and normal care but cut back and rest from October to January. Grow from seed or half-ripened tip cuttings.

AMAZON LILY
Eucharis grandiflora

Blossoms of snow white which give off a subtle, lemony fragrance may crown these tropical American beauties several times yearly. Average house humidity and temperature (but slightly cooler during the fall), a semi-sunny location, and a rich, evenly moist soil are necessities. Divide and repot with new soil every three years. Propagate by seeds in early spring, or by offshoots when repotting.

ARTILLERY PLANT
Pilea microphylla

This delightful, light green succulent comes from tropical America. It usually grows to a medium height, and rarely grows beyond 15 inches. Tiny clusters of flowers grace this fern-like plant at the leaf axils. These blossoms release puffs of pollen dust when disturbed or touched. An ideal plant for an east or west window box, the artillery plant tolerates partial sun, but it prefers strong light. Do not allow the soil to become dry, but beware of over watering. Propagate by cuttings, which root very easily.

AURORA BOREALIS PLANT
Kalanchoe fedtschenkoi marginata

The edges of the bluish-green leaves of this unusual kalanchoe will change color depending upon the amount of light the plant receives. Remaining white in partial shade, they will blush a lovely shade of pink when given the benefit of full sun. The deep coral-to-pink flowers will last for several months (mid-winter to spring) if there is sufficient sunshine. Give it a sandy soil with good drainage. Do not over water, but limp foliage is a sign of under watering. It will thrive despite a dry atmosphere. Propagate by planting six-inch cuttings.

AZALEA
Rhododendron

Originally from the cooler areas of the Northern Hemisphere, these woody, small- to medium-sized plants are quite adaptable to the indoor life. However, a cool, sunny, moist locale is a must if this perennial is to thrive indoors. Spray the plants every day and keep the soil moist to insure the proper humidity. Blossoms usually appear in late winter and should continue to thrive for several weeks if proper care is taken. When blossoms begin to fade, use an acid-type fertilizer every four weeks until the summer. You may relocate azaleas in your outdoor garden in the summer if you have a semi-shady, sheltered area. They will require a high humus content soil enriched with peat moss and sand. Re-

member to keep the plants moist, but not soggy, in the summer and feed every two weeks. Repot with fresh, acidic soil every year.

BOXWOOD
Buxus microphylla japonica

This small evergreen shrub was originally grown in Africa and southern Europe. It is a favorite for adding interest and charm to a miniature dish garden or window box. The dense and compact plant with its rich green foliage can provide excellent variety and contrast when used with feathery ferns and soft begonias. Boxwood is a slow grower, but it does need plenty of sun (moderate direct light) and a cool temperature. It also thrives on light watering, and the soil should be well drained. Fertilize about twice a year. Keep boxwood pruned to maintain the compact, well-rounded appearance.

BRAZILIAN EDELWEISS
Rechsteineria leucotricha

A charming house guest from South America that is an abundant, almost continuous bloomer. The grayish, fuzzy leaves are accented by tubular, rose-pink blossoms that grow from the leaf axils. Brazilian edelweiss requires full sun, warmth, and high humidity. Mist frequently, and keep soil moist but not soggy. Since this is a low, trailing plant, it should be pruned from time to time to preserve its shape. Fertilize at least once a month, except when the plant is dormant in the autumn.

CALLA LILY
Zantedeschia aethiopica

Gorgeous, white flowers adorn this South African beauty in the winter and spring. They grow to a height of about two to four feet and are quite adaptable to ordinary house conditions. Calla lilies require abundant light, moisture, fertilizer, and they prefer moderate warmth. Start your calla lilies from bulbs in August and you should have blooms in October. You may want to use a separate container for each bloom. Use a pot about six inches in diameter for each bulb and soil of loam, peat, and sand in equal parts. Plant your bulbs approximately one-and-one-half to two inches deep and leave in a cool, dark locale for about a month. Relocate to a sunny area and begin to water and fertilize every two or three days. Gradually decrease the amount of water and food when the blooms are finished. Leave the bulbs in the dry pots until the following August when you can repot with fresh soil.

CHRISTMAS CACTUS
Schlumbergera bridgesii

This popular plant has bright red flowers which normally last for weeks. For best results, you should place your Christmas cactus on a window sill which gets full sunlight. Water infrequently during the summer and begin to increase the amount and frequency in early September to promote the magnificent blooms for the Christmas season. The soil should be sandy or gravelly. To propagate, break off a three- to eight-inch piece of branch and root it in about two inches of soil in another pot. Do not crowd the plants. They will root readily and grow naturally into low, full, trailing beauties.

CORAL PLANT
Jatropha multifida

A New World, recent addition to the legion of house plants. The coral red flowers, which bloom almost continuously dramatically accent the roundish, lobed leaves. Give it a sunny exposure and the temperature and humidity of a normal house environment. The soil should be kept evenly moist at all times. Propagate by seeds or by cutting firm, young branches, allowing them to dry slightly, and rooting them.

CORDUROY PLANT
Hoffmania refulgens

The closely placed, slightly depressed, parallel veins and fuzzy texture of the leaves give this plant its name. The upper, broad end of the leaves is usually green, copper, or rose in color, while the veins range from light green, to pink, or silver. Give it average house temperatures, high humidity, and a semi-shady exposure. Keep soil evenly moist at all times. Propagates easily by cuttings placed in moist soil and kept warm. Native to Mexico.

DWARF CENTURY PLANT
Agave miradorensis

A formidable-looking and extremely hardy plant from Mexico. Wide, short grayish-green leaves are symmetrically arranged in a rosette shape. The tough and fibrous leaves are edged with sharp, spine-like projections. Average house temperatures and humidity, little water, and a sunny exposure are its only necessities. Water only when the soil is dry to the touch. Propagate by offsets throughout the year.

FATSHEDERA
Fatshedera lizei

Often called "tree ivy" this shrub is a cross between Engligh ivy and fatsia, which are both of the same family. It is an erect plant, with thick evergreen leaves similar to those of an ivy. It may need support to remain upright, since it has a weak stem. It requires an east or west exposure, a cool temperature, a fertile, humus-rich, evenly moist soil. One of its varieties has dark green leaves with a sharply contrasting, cream-white marking along each leaf edge. You can propagate fatshedera by cuttings which root very easily.

FATSIA
Fatsia japonica

This handsome, tall foliage plant was originally grown in Japan. The glossy, dark green, maple-like leaves can provide an exotic, highly decorative, tropical accent when arranged properly. It grows best in an east or west exposure, and requires an evenly moist soil of sand, loam, and peat moss in equal parts. Do not let your fatsia become too warm and keep it in an area where the air circulates to prevent red spider mite infestation. Fatsia can be propagated from cuttings in the spring. Pot the plants in a large container and give them plenty of room to grow. They often reach a height of up to 15 feet. Repot whenever necessary.

FLOWERING MAPLE
Abutilon hybridium

Often called a Chinese bellflower, this small tree originated in South America. The hanging, bell-like flowers resemble old fashioned hoop dresses and come in colors ranging from white to red, pink, apricot, and yellow. The maple-like, white-rimmed leaves can dominate the plant at the expense of the delicate blooms if proper care is not taken. To prevent this, do not fertilize, keep potbound, and prune in the winter. Your flowering maple should do well in a south or west exposure. It requires a fairly moist, not soggy soil, which can be slightly less moist in the winter months. To propagate, take branch tips of four to six inches from the original plant. Root them in moist sand or rooting medium to a depth of about one to two inches.

GERMAN IVY
Senecio mikaniodies

This popular climbing plant is also called "water ivy" and "parlor ivy." The thin, bright green leaves and slender stems resemble fragile English ivy and do well in hanging planters. It is a fast grower and propagates easily by cuttings. Average house temperatures and humidity, and a feeding every six weeks are its moderate requirements. German ivy should have a sunny winter exposure and a partial-shade summer exposure. Allow the soil to dry between waterings.

HIBISCUS

Hibiscus rosa-sinensis

The rose-of-China comes in many different varieties. It has been selected as the official flower of the State of Hawaii. Although it is an outdoor bush, it is ideally suited to an indoor life. The hibiscus usually begins to put out blooms when it is only a few inches high, and it should continue to bloom almost constantly when properly cared for. The flowers usually remain open for only a day, with few varieties lasting any longer. It is a slow grower, although it is a tall plant, often reaching a height of about two feet. Noted for its spectacular blooms resembling hollyhocks, the blooms may be single or double, ranging in shades from yellow to salmon, pink, and red. Full sunlight, plenty of moisture, and average house temperatures are necessities. The soil should be equal parts of peat moss, sand, and loam and should be kept evenly moist, especially when the plant is budding or blooming. Plants must be fertilized weekly when active. Repot in the spring, when roots and leaves may be pruned. Propagate by taking a four-inch stem cutting and rooting it, making sure it is kept constantly moist.

HYDRANGEA

Hydrangea macrophylla

A popular gift at Easter and Mother's Day, the "snowball bush" is a shrub with large leaves and clusters of pink, white, or blue flowers. The large, snowball-shaped flower clusters and the thin, papery leaves require a constantly moist, almost wet, soil. Blooms will last for about six weeks in the spring if kept in a cool, humid locale. When blossoms fade, prune to about half the original size. Repot in equal parts of loam, peat moss, and sand. During the summer, keep watered and fed. In winter, keep in a cool, dark place with just enough water to prevent withering of the stems. Relocate to a semi-sunny, warmer, humid locale in early January.

IMPATIENS

Impatiens

An old-fashioned favorite often referred to as a "patience plant" or "patient Lucy." It is succulently-stemmed with fleshy foliage. When properly cared for, it will bloom year-round in shades of red, white, pink, or coral. Grows easily from seeds and can also be rooted from the garden in late summer. It requires average soil and full sun during the winter and an east or west exposure during the summer. Water frequently, but let the soil almost dry once every two weeks. Fertilize every two-and-one-half weeks when active. It is ideal as a hanging basket plant, but it can also be pruned to maintain a more compact shape. Originally from the mountainous regions of New Guinea and Africa.

KAFIR LILY

Clivia miniata

This handsome evergreen comes from South Africa. It is exceptionally attractive when in bloom, but only mature plants do so. Between 12 and 15 fragrant, trumpet-shaped blossoms, which range in color from yellow to orange, salmon, and scarlet, usually appear in the spring. Kafir lilies require good light, but never hot sun. They usually grow to a height of about two feet, so give them plenty of room. Keeping them pot-bound and undivided encourages flowering. Repot only when the plant becomes too large to handle, about every four years. The soil should dry before rewatering, but do not let the leaves wilt. Keep the soil moist when the plant is budding or blooming.

LILY OF THE VALLEY

Convallaria majalis

A hardy, generally outdoor plant, the lily of the valley can be grown as a temporary, accent addition indoors. A low-growing plant, it has a single, one-sided spike of tiny, bell-shaped, white flowers growing between graceful, light green leaves. Specially treated roots, or pips, are available in the fall from commercial growers. Keep the plants about one-and-one-half inches apart, evenly moist, and in a cool, sunny place. Flowers should appear in about three weeks. Do not attempt to transplant the untreated pips from an outdoor garden.

LITHOPS

Lithops

The unusual appearance of these small South African succulents accounts for their popular names, "living stone" and "stone face." Each plant has a pair of fleshy leaves which are set close together and resemble a small, split rock or stone. Large white, yellow or orange blossoms may appear, usually after August. When the blossoms fade the plant will rest for a time. They prefer dry, sunny locations, and a rather sandy soil. Water sparingly, especially during the winter. Propagate by seeds in the early spring.

PANDA PLANT

Kalanchoe tomentosa

The thick, firm, light grayish-green leaves of the panda plant seem to be covered in fur or felt. Leaf tips are decorated with brown markings. Its velvety texture makes it ideal for adding interest to any window-box display. Originally from Madagascar, the panda plant requires lots of sun in the autumn and winter. It can do quite well in the spring and summer in a semi-shady location. During its active time (autumn and winter) water copiously, but let the soil dry before rewatering. Water lightly at other times. Good drainage is essential. Propagate by breaking off a leaf or stem. Let the cut edge dry, then place in filtered sun, in about half an inch of sand. Do not over water. Move to a sunnier location and increase water when leaf plumps up again.

PURPLE HEART

Setcreasea purpurea

A Mexican import with fleshy, sword-shaped leaves that appear purple in bright sunlight. Tiny lilac flowers bloom between the leaves during the summer and autumn. Will do well given the temperature and humidity levels of the average house, but does require a constantly moist soil. Keep it out of direct sun during the late summer months. Propagate by offsets or by transplanting the seedlings which may appear.

SCREW PINE

Pandanus

This tropical shrub is often cultivated as a foliage plant. A native of Polynesia, it is not a true pine. Long, sword-shaped leaves with finely serrated edges grow in a perfect spiral arrangement. Screw pine flourishes in high humidity, and a rich, well-drained soil. Give it a warm area near an east or west exposure. Keep the soil evenly moist, except in the autumn months when it can remain slightly drier. Its most active time is usually mid- to late-winter, continuing to summer. Repot when necessary during this active period.

STARFISH FLOWER

Stapelia

A succulent member of the milkwood family characterized by five-petaled flowers and erect, spiny stems. Most varieties, especially the larger-flowered ones, have an unpleasant odor. It requires heat and full sun. The soil should be evenly, but not overly, moist in the summer and drier in the winter. Limp stems indicate the need for more water. Propagate in late spring or summer by breaking off a two-inch piece of the stem and rooting it in another pot.

STEPHANOTIS

Stephanotis floribunda

A delicate twiner which is most abundant in June and extremely popular with brides. White, waxy clusters of tubular flowers contrast with the glossy, oblong-shaped, deep green leaves. Average house temperatures and humidity, an evenly moist soil, and a sunny exposure are the basic requirements. Fertilize biweekly. In winter, cease fertilizing, reduce the amount of water, and relocate to an area with slightly lower temperatures. Propagate in spring by rooting half-mature stem pieces in moist soil in a warm place.

SWEET POTATO

Ipomoea batatas

A beautiful and easy-to-grow vine that is especially well-suited to hanging planters. Originally from the East Indies, most potatoes that are available commercially have been treated to prevent buds from sprouting. If, however, you can find a potato that has not been treated, or is already sprouting, it will easily root. Place a whole potato in a warm, bright location with its lower half submerged in water. Change the water as often as necessary to keep it fresh. Within three weeks sprouts, and soon leaves and vine-like growth, will appear. Continue to grow the plant in water, or transplant it to a moisture-retaining planting medium. Be careful to keep the medium evenly moist at all times.

TEMPLE BELLS

Smithiantha

Scarlet and yellow bell-like flowers emerge from the top of magnificent foliage. Dark green, heart-shaped leaves appear to be covered in red velvet. It is a richly textured and extraordinarily beautiful plant, especially when blooming, November to April. From the tropics of Mexico and Guatemala, it requires high humidity, warm temperatures, and daily misting. Keep the soil moist while budding and blooming. When blossoms fade, gradually decrease the amount and frequency of watering. Leave the plants in near-dry soil and permit them to rest in a dark place for about three months. Propagate temple bells by planting seeds in spring or rhizomes in summer. Fertilize about once a week while growing.

TI PLANT

Cordyline terminalis

A mature crown of palm-like leaves in colors that range from red, maroon, and pink, to deep green top a cane-like stalk or stem. A fast grower, it can reach a height of about ten feet when grown outdoors in a warm climate. Indoors, average house temperatures and humidity, a moist soil, and an east or west exposure are required. Propagate by rooting one-inch pieces of the stem in a moist, sandy soil. Native to India and the islands of the South Pacific.

Propagation

There is a lot of fun and pleasure, and a feeling of satisfaction, in propagating a favorite plant to give someone as a living gift, or to increase the number of plant people in your home.

Seed or cuttings?

A number of simple techniques can be used with ease to propagate plants in the home. The only tools needed are a sharp pocket knife and a pair of small pruning shears.

Methods of propagation are divided into two basic categories: sexual (using seeds), and vegetative (using parts of one plant to grow other plants).

The method selected, seed or cuttings, will usually be related to the plant, because some can be propagated by one means and not the other, and some by both. If seed and vegetative means are both useable for a particular plant, then consider the other points involved.

Growing plants from seeds can result in some variability in the new plants because each seed will have half of the male parent's characteristics and half of the female parent's characteristics.

Some plants produce large quantities of seeds, others very few. Some plants require hand pollination from the male flower to the female flower at the right time. The home plant grower may find crossing of plants a very fulfilling hobby.

Plantings grown from cuttings completely resemble the plant from which they were taken. They are totally a child of the source plant.

Propagating structures

An important problem in propagating plants by seed or cuttings is maintaining a high moisture level in the air. Some kind of simple structure is needed that keeps moisture in but allows air circulation.

For cuttings try using 8-inch plastic pots. Close the drainage hole at the bottom of the pot with clay or putty and fill the pot with vermiculite or perlite. Then take a 2- or 3-inch pot and close the drainage hole as before. The small pot is then placed in the center of the large pot and filled with water. Cuttings are planted in the moistened medium in the larger pot.

Blocks of plastic foam can also be used to root cuttings. Dampen the block and wrap the top

The smaller, inner clay pot contains water. The clay is porous, allowing the water to seep through to the soil of the larger pot which contains fresh plant cuttings.

Blocks of plastic foam can be used for rooting cuttings. The block should be thoroughly wet (right), wrapped in foil (center), and the cuttings inserted (left).

and sides in aluminum foil. Then use a scissors to cut slits in the foam and insert the cuttings in these. As the foam dries out, add more water to keep it moist.

A round or square aquarium makes a very neat propagating unit for both seeds and cuttings. The bottom should be covered with about an inch of gravel for drainage, topped with 3 to 4 inches of vermiculite or perlite. When the media is moistened, seeds can be sown or cuttings placed in position. A piece of glass or polyethylene placed over the top completes the propagating structure. If light is desired, a small aquarium lamp can be used, with an incandescent tube of 25 watts or less, with a glass top **only.**

Simple propagating mini-greenhouses can be made using large freezer bags of polyethylene. An inch of pebbles is first put into the bag and then three inches or so of vermiculite or potting mix. After water is added and either seeds planted or cuttings placed, the bags are fastened carefully without disturbing the cuttings. The completed mini-greenhouse can be placed on a window with a northern exposure. No further watering is needed until the seeds are germinated or the cuttings examined after eight weeks.

Cuttings will usually root in from eight to ten weeks. After eight weeks gently open the bag and remove a cutting. If a number of roots ½- to 1-inch long have formed the cutting is ready to be potted.

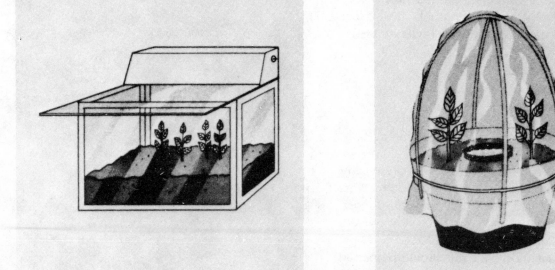

(Left) An aquarium with a glass top makes an excellent propagating unit. A 25-watt fluorescent tube provides extra light.
(Right) Bent metal hangers are placed over the top of a container and a plastic bag or sheet is slipped over the frame and tied in place.

A plastic bag is prepared to receiving cuttings by filling it with a one-inch layer of pebbles and several inches of vermiculite. Dampen the medium and set the seeds or cuttings in place.

The mini-greenhouse plastic bag is sealed and placed in a cool window where it will receive partial sunlight.

Before potting, however, condition the plants to room humidity by keeping the bag open for increasing periods of time during a week. Keep the soil mixture moist during this period. Any cuttings which have not rooted, but are still alive, should be kept in the closed plastic bag, and examined every two weeks for roots. Any cuttings which have lost their leaves or decayed at the base should be tossed out.

Rooting media

There is virtually no limit to the combination of materials that can be used for rooting cuttings and germinating seeds.

The major materials, all of which are readily found in garden stores as well as many supermarkets and five-and-tens, are sand, soil, sphagnum moss, peat moss, vermiculite and perlite. The last two are sterile when bought.

Fibrous peat moss and soil should be passed through a coarse screen to remove larger particles, twigs and stones. The next step is to mix the peat

The cutting shown is ready for transplanting. It has well-formed roots that are from one-half to one inch in length.

with sand and soil in a ratio you find best. Try using parts of each of these components.

The moist mixture can be sterilized at 180°F. in a metal pan in the oven for one-half hour. When the mix is cooled, add vermiculite or perlite in any amount you feel best.

When the mix is ready, add water and combine well. The soil is ready for use when you squeeze a handful and only a few drops of water squeeze out. Be careful in handling the hot sand, soil or mixes and containers as they can cause severe burns. Use a hot pad for safety.

Clay pots, and ceramic jugs and aquariums made of a single piece of glass, can be sterilized in the same way. For plastic containers, rinse with boiling water, followed by a thorough scrubbing with soap and water and a series of cold water rinses.

Hormones

Plant hormones are available at garden stores

Proper preparation of your potting mix includes careful sifting of the soil and sand.

Water the potting mix before using it. It should be thoroughly moist, but not soggy.

Healthy plant specimens make healthy cuttings. Stems should be firm and snap crisply.

and flower shops to help stimulate root formation. The end of a cutting or stem of a leaf is dipped in water, then into the hormone powder, and the excess knocked off by gently tapping the cutting.

Cuttings

A cutting is a piece of an older plant such as a stem, leaf or root used to produce a new plant exactly like the parent plant. The procedure usually begins with the separation of the selected plant part from the parent. The exception is air-layering, which will be discussed later.

Most house plants usually can be readily propagated by cuttings. Success in rooting cuttings depends on the survival of the cuttings until they grow roots and leaves, and keeping them from dying until these growths appear.

Material selected for cuttings should be healthy and free from insect and disease damage. It should be taken from plants that have no flowers because plants in flower do not root easily.

A quick and simple way of testing material if you have enough is to snap a piece of stem be-

tween your fingers. A crisp popping sound indicates the material is ready for rooting.

Kinds of cuttings

Leaf, stem and canes are the sources of materials for cuttings.

Stem cuttings or slips are made from strong lateral or terminal shoots. Plants propagated by this method include everblooming begonia, cactus, coleus, German ivy, philodendron and wax plants. A good stem cutting is 3 to 6 inches long. Using a sharp knife, cut at a slight angle just below the node, or joints, in the stem. Remove the leaves from the bottom 2 or 3 inches and insert in the rooting medium.

Leaf bud cuttings are made by cutting a segment of stem with a leaf and the bud in the axil of the leaf. The cutting is planted horizontally below the surface of the propagating media. Philodendron, pothos, wax plant are among those propagated this way.

Cane cuttings are made from the cane-like

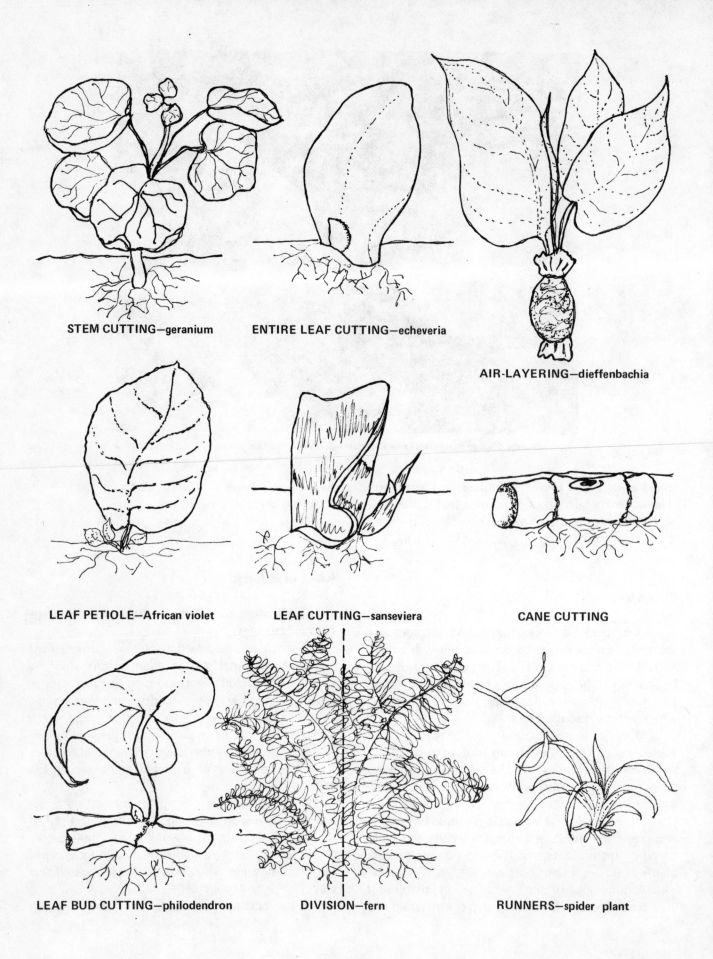

STEM CUTTING—geranium

ENTIRE LEAF CUTTING—echeveria

AIR-LAYERING—dieffenbachia

LEAF PETIOLE—African violet

LEAF CUTTING—sansevieria

CANE CUTTING

LEAF BUD CUTTING—philodendron

DIVISION—fern

RUNNERS—spider plant

stems that are found at the base of certain plants after the older leaves drop off. These canes are cut into pieces with two leaf scars per piece. The cutting is planted horizontally just below the soil surface, with the dormant eye facing upward. Chinese evergreen, dracaena, and dumb cane can be handled in this way.

An entire leaf is used for stonecrop, hen-and-chickens, and snake plant. Snake plant and the palmleaf begonia can be cut into two to four sections and used to produce several plants.

Division

A number of plants form clumps, such as ferns, snake plant, some African violets, prayer plant, English ivy and everblooming begonia. These clumps can be separated into several smaller plants.

Be sure to leave as much soil as possible on the roots during the operation.

Air-layering

Air-layering is spectacular but not too difficult a technique to master. It is used with woody stemmed plants such as the rubber plant, croton, fiddleleaf fig and schefflera.

A one-year-old stem is cut halfway through and the cut held open with a small wedge, or the bark is scraped ½-inch wide around the stem. Moist sphagnum moss is tied in a ball around the cut. Friction tape is used to bind the plastic to make an airtight package the size of an orange or large apple. New roots will form in the plastic ball; when you can see them, cut the plant off below the new root area and pot.

A leaf bud cutting which has been properly planted.

Some plants, such as African violets, have multiple crowns, or growing points, which can be divided and nurtured into several complete plants.

velop sufficiently to permit cutting the "umbilical" cord of the runner from the mother plant to the young plant.

The second method is to cut off the leafy cluster with a portion of the runner and root it.

Tap water

The top of a carrot or a piece of sweet potato could be grown into a miraculous plant all of your own. Using tap water you can make a series of bottle gardens that give hours of enjoyment for free.

Almost any kind of container can be used as long as it is waterproof. Bottles and jars of any shape and size will do well. A large number of plants can be propagated in this way.

Plants which can be propagated in water.

African violet	grape ivy
aglaonema	hibiscus
aluminum plant	impatiens
aucuba	ivy
avocado	peperomia
carrot	philodendron
coleus	sweet potato
geranium	wax begonia

The successful fruits of your labors. Five separate African violet plants have been obtained from the primary plant.

This method can be used to reshape tall leggy plants which have lost their bottom leaves. The air-layering is done right below the remaining leaves and the ungainly stem is cut back to 8 or 10 inches. New shoots will grow to make a more attractive plant and you will then have two plants.

Runners

Runners are shoots or stems which grow along the surface of the ground and which often produce clusters of leaves at their nodes, or joints.

Among the house plants which produce runners are strawberry geranium, spider plant, Boston fern, mother-of-thousands, apostle plant and piggyback plant.

When a plant produces runners, fill several flower pots with your favorite prepared soil mix. Place each leafy cluster on the soil in one of the pots. Then use an open, non-spring clothes pin, crossed wooden matches or toothpicks to hold the runner in place. Keep the soil moist and the pot in subdued light. In about a month roots should de-

This woody-stemmed plant is being properly prepared for air-layering. A wedge will now be inserted in the cut.

Moist sphagnum is wrapped around the cut and loosely tied to keep it in place.

The next step: a piece of plastic is wrapped around the moist sphagnum moss.

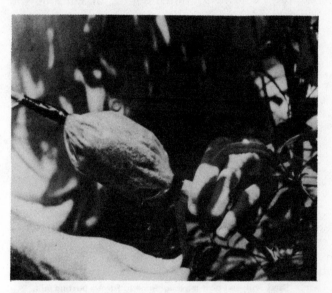

The plastic "cocoon" is now secured in place. Some friction tape comes in handy at this point.

The first step is to wash the container with hot, soapy tap water, then rinse several times and fill the bottle to an inch or two of the top. Then cut a small branch or stem from the mother plant with a sharp knife just below the point at which a leaf grows. Next cut off the top of the cutting, leaving a stem about 8 to 12 inches long, and put in the water. If leaves extend under water, remove them.

Keep the water level at its original height and once a month wash the bottles well to reduce algae growth. Rotate the container in the light to encourage uniform growth.

Seeds

A large number of house plants can be propagated by sexual means from seed. The list includes African violet, begonia, cacti, coleus, cyclamen, fuchsia, gloxinia and a great many more.

Seed can be bought for many of these and in some cases can be obtained at home. Garden club members often trade seeds with each other, a worthwhile program activity.

Growing plants from seed is a longer process than growing them by vegetative methods. However, it is an easy way to grow a larger number than

Several cuttings can be propagated in each bottle of water.

Containers

Flats of wood, flower pots or trays of heat-proof material 3 to 4 inches deep can be used to germinate seed. If pots are used the drainage hole should be covered to keep the soil from running out. A piece of broken pot or some large pieces of gravel will do well if you have them handy.

If you are using seed flats cover the bottom with 4 or 5 sheets of newspaper to keep the soil

is possible from a limited source of cuttings and runners. Using seed makes it practical for a plant enthusiast to start several pots of seed in late summer or early fall in order to give young plants to friends and guests during the December holiday season.

Soil mixture

Much the same materials used for cuttings are used for seeds. Variations are an individual matter based on personal preference. Sterilization follows the same procedure.

Sand, soil, and peat moss combine to form a potting mix.

A plaque of pressed peat moss can take the place of a soil mix. Just moisten it and add the seed.

mix from running out. Plastic flats or trays do not require this step. The containers are treated as for cuttings to keep them as free of disease as it possible.

Small plaques of pressed peat moss can be used very satisfactorily. Put one of the plaques into a styrofoam cup and then add sufficient water to swell the plaque. After about half an hour drain off the excess water and plant the seeds. A small sandwich bag completes this mini-propagating contrivance.

Planting

The container is filled to within ½-inch of the top with the soil mix, and then pressed down firmly with the knuckles and the thumbs along the edges. Sprinkle about ¼-inch of fine vermiculite over the surface. Moisten the soil by placing the container in a shallow pan of water until the vermiculite is moist or use a fine sprinkler from the top. If any deep depressions appear, fill them up and pack down again.

Once the vermiculite is moist, make slight depressions 1/8-inch to ¼-inch deep in one or more rows in the surface of the soil. Each depression or row, if you make several, should be about 2 inches from its neighbor.

Using your hands, firmly press the potting mix into the container to prevent its packing down when moistened.

Sow the seeds by gently tapping the seed packet with the forefinger so that the seeds are somewhat scattered in the row. If the seeds are sown too close together the seedlings will be spindly and weak.

Small seeds such as African violet and begonia are left uncovered as they are likely not to germinate if they are covered. Larger seeds are covered with vermiculite or screened sphagnum moss until they are just hidden and gently pressed down so the seeds are in contact with the soil. Last, cover the container with a polyethylene plastic freezer

Use a bulb sprayer or sprinkler to moisten the mix.

bag to minimize moisture loss. No further water should be needed until the bag is removed.

Seedling care

The container may be placed in a window sill out of the direct rays of the sun. The best temperature range is 65-75°F.

Some plants, like coleus and geraniums, are sun lovers and from a week after the plastic is removed they should be kept in direct sun. Others, such as African violet and begonia, thrive in bright light but not direct sun.

As soon as the first leaves are formed the plastic bag can be removed and the seedlings trans-

To assure even distribution when sowing seeds, hold the pack in one hand and gently tap the pack with the other.

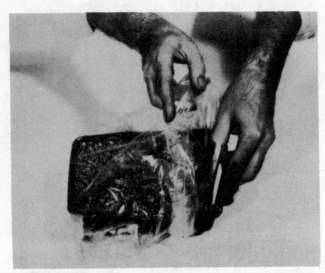

Enclosing the flat or pot in a plastic bag will keep the soil evenly moist without constantly rewatering.

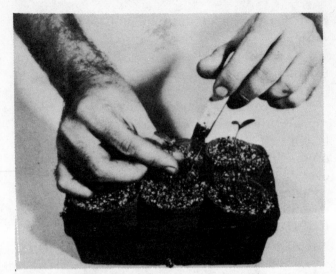

When the seedlings form true leaves they are ready to be transplanted into three-inch pots.

planted either one to a 3-inch pot, or several to a flat, using your own favorite soil mixture.

Be sure the plants are well watered but not to the point where the water runs out of the bottom of the container.

Special methods for some cacti and succulents

Although most cacti and succulents can be propagated readily by seed, there are some vegetative methods worth considering.

Offsets

Offsets are plants produced by other plants. Sometimes these new plants are produced on the body of the older plants, as with *Echinocereus* and *Echinopsis.* In other plants, including *Agave, Aloe, Sedum* and *Haworthia,* a circle of young plants is produced around the base of the mother plant attached by their roots. Some offsets are produced on leaves as is found on *Bryophyllum.* Any such offsets can be separated from the parent plant and potted.

Cuttings

Leaves of *Aloe, Sedum,* and others can be used to propagate new plants. Carefully cut off a healthy leaf, lay it on a pot of sand and peg it down along the edges using toothpicks. The leaf will gradually dry up and a new plant appear at the point where the leaf had been attached to the old plant. Branching succulents and cacti can be propagated by cuttings made of parts of the branches and trunks.

Some of the *Euphorbias, Opuntias,* and *Echevarias* can be propagated by simply cutting a piece of a branch and putting it into a suitable rooting medium. Other cacti, including the *Echevaria* and the *Cereus,* can be propagated by cutting off the top of the stem and placing it in sand. Such cut tops produce series of plantlets which in turn can be potted.

All cuttings should be kept in a cool, well ventilated place for three or four days after cutting and before potting to encourage callus formation, the soft tissue which forms over the cut surface of a stem from which the new roots develop.

114

Terrariums; Gardening in Glass

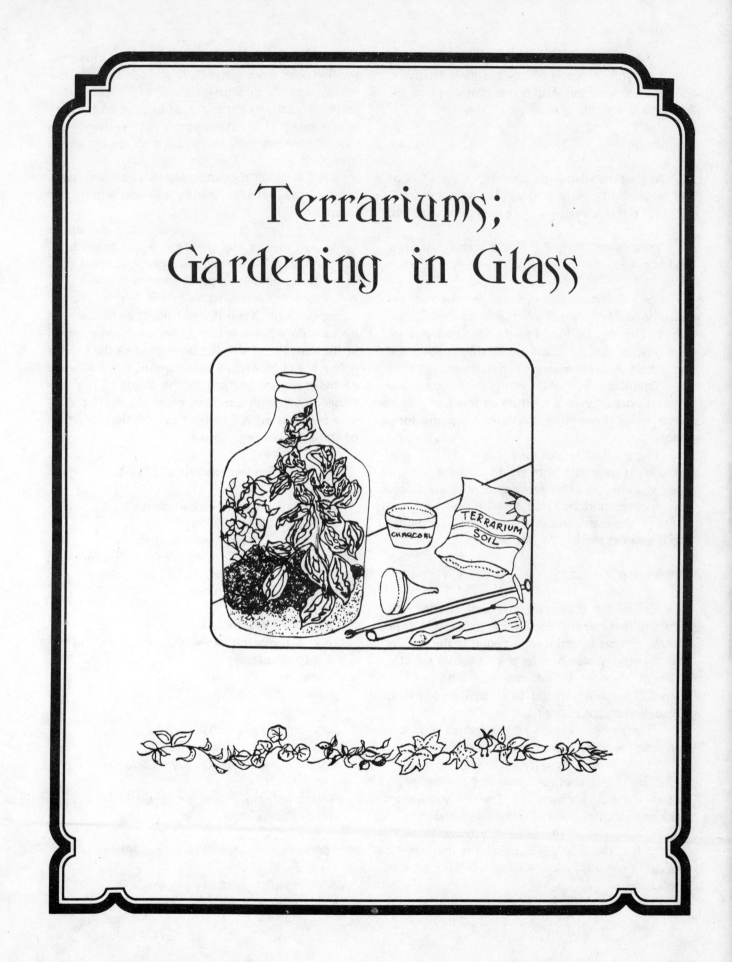

To transport an entire ecosystem, in miniature, into your home is one of the most satisfying and pleasing activities with plants that we know of. And that is what terrariums are all about.

Equipment

A **glass container** to permit passage of light and for visibility. Anything of glass with a top will do. If no top is available a piece of plastic wrap will serve.

Suitable soil mix. For desert scenes fine river sand is needed, or desert sand if you have a desert handy.

For a forest scene of mosses, lichens and ecologically similar plants, an organic soil mix is required. This can be found in the forest, if you are near one, or can be made by mixing ½ good soil and ½ humus, dried manure or peat moss.

Drainage. Pebbles, small rocks, charcoal, broken pots or even a mixture of these to include some twigs, leaves and the litter from the forest floor.

Plants. Just about any plant if it is small enough. If several plants are to be used, be sure they require the same growing conditions. Cactus and moss would be strange bedfellows. A list of some of the many suitable plants for glass gardening is given at the end of this chapter.

Preparation

Be sure the container is well cleaned, particularly if it has had food in it. If it is a food jar, remove the cardboard usually found in the lid.

First, lay down a layer of pebbles or other drainage material to prevent waterlogging of the plants. This layer would be 1 to 2 inches deep, depending on the container size.

Next, line the sides of the container (except for desert scenes) with 1-inch strips of moss found on flat stones and old logs, green side out.

Then place about 2 inches of your soil mix on top of the drainage materials. The mix you use will vary with experience but try to approximate the soil in which your plants usually grow. Slope the soil higher towards the back of the container to present a natural look and avoid a flat formal looking surface.

Very carefully place the plants in position with larger ones to the back so as not to block the smaller ones from view. Do not pack them in too closely and be sure they do not touch each other or the sides of the container, at least when they are first planted. If the container is narrow-mouthed a pair of tweezers may be required to get the plants into position.

A few small rocks to resemble boulders, carefully placed between plants, will add a touch of beauty.

Once planting is complete, spray the plants lightly with water and then add water gently until the soil is wet, but not waterlogged. Clean the sides of the terrarium with a paper towel and cover.

Place the container in bright light but not in direct sunlight. Keep the soil moist as needed but be sure no water appears in the drainage material at the bottom. If this happens, remove the top for a few hours to permit evaporation. If small beads of moisture accumulate on the inside of the container your terrarium is in good shape. If the inside becomes misted, permit evaporation to get rid of the excess water.

Some Recommended Wild Plants

bloodroot, *Sanguinaria canadensis*
cinquefoil, *Potentilla* spp.
club moss, *Lycopodium clavatum*
dogtooth violet, *Erythronium grandiflorum*
Dutchman's breeches, *Dicentra cucullaria*
evergreens, such as pines
ferns, small
goldthread, *Coptis* spp.
jack in the pulpit, *Arisaema triphyllum* and
    related species
lichens, any
liverleaf, *Hepatica* spp.
mosses, any
partridgeberry, *Mitchella repens*
pipsissewa, *Chimaphila umbellata*
rattlesnake plantain, *Goodyera pubescens*
violet, *Viola* spp.
wild strawberry, *Fragaria virginiana*
wintergreen, *Gaultheria procumbens*

Some Recommended Cultivated Plants

African violet, *Saintpauli ionantha*
artillary plant, *Pilea microphylla*

An elegantly-shaped glass container with a matching lid makes an ideal setting for a forest scene of ferns.

A food jar makes a utilitarian, but excellent terrarium for several small plants. The top can be covered with plastic wrap.

A brandy snifter makes a good terrarium. This one even has its own plastic lid.

baby's tears, *Helxine* spp.
begonia, *Begonia foliosa, B. imperalis*
bibergia, *Bibergia nutans*
calathea, *Calathea illustris, C. rose-picta,*
    C. zebrina
Chinese evergreen, *Aglaonema commutatum,*
    A. costatum
coleus, *Coleus* spp.
creeping fig, *Ficus punila*
croton, *Codiaeum* spp.
dracaena, *Dracaena godseffiana, D. goldieana,*
    D. sanderiana
dumb cane, *Dieffenbachia seguine*
earth-star, *Crypthanthus bivittatus, C. zonatus*
English ivy, *Hedera helix*
fittonia, *Fittonia vershaffelti, F. vershaffelti*
    var. *argyroneura*

flamingo flower, *Anthurium scherzerianum*
friendship plant, *Pilea involucrata*
gold-dust plant, *Aucuba japonica*
grape ivy, *Cissus rhombifolia*
Joseph's coat, *Amaranthus tricolor*
orchids, small
palms, small
peperomia, *Peperomia* spp.
Philodendron, *Philodendron cordatum,*
    P. micans
pothos, *Scindapsus pictus* var. *argyraeus*
prayer plant, *Maranta arundinacea* var.
    variegata, M. Leucomerua var.
selaginella, *Selaginella* spp.
snake plant, *Sansevieria* spp.
wandering Jew, *Tradescantia fluminesis,* and
    Zebrina pendula

Forcing Bulbs

The advent of fall and cold weather is no reason to forego the pleasures that so many bulbs can provide indoors.

Bright colors, sometimes a soul-lifting fragrance, a forecast of the spring, are all at your command with a fairly simple technique.

A revival in bulb forcing at home, in schools and in offices is in full swing. Bulb forcing is simply the method used to make them bloom indoors without waiting for spring.

Bulbs for forcing can be bought in the fall. Select large healthy bulbs of the variety you have decided you want. Tulip bulbs should be over 1½ inches in diameter. This list will be of use.

Bulbs for forcing

Tender
    amaryllis
    narcissus
Hardy
    crocus
    daffodil
    grape hyacinth
    hyacinth
    jonquil
    snowdrops
    Darwin tulips
    early tulips
    triumph tulips

If you get your bulbs before you are ready to plant them, they can be stored in a well ventilated location at 55-60°F. for several weeks. Planting may be done between October and December 1.

Containers

There are few limits as to the kind of containers you may use. The container should be shallow, not more than 6 to 8 inches deep. For paperwhite narcissus a container 3 inches deep is fine. For tulips, hyacinths and daffodils a depth of 6 inches is suitable.

Good drainage is as important for bulbs as it is for any other plant. Provide an inch of pebbles at the bottom of the container, or even better, a drainage hole.

Soil mixes and media

Two mixes are recommended: No. 1 for hardy bulbs, and No. 2 for tender bulbs. The soil mix should come to ½ inch of the top of the pot.

No. 1 — 1/3 peat moss, 1/3 rich soil and 1/3 leaf mold.

No. 2 — 2/3 rich soil and 1/3 sand.

A third potting material can be made of inert materials such as pebbles, vermiculite or perlite. These are used for growing daffodils and paperwhite narcissus. Water can also serve as a growth media and is often used for forcing hyacinths.

Planting bulbs

Use only one kind of bulb for each container.

Plant hyacinths 3 or 4 to a 6-inch pot or one to a 4-inch pot, with the bulb tops showing above the soil.

Plant 3 tulip bulbs to a 5-inch container and 6 to 9 tulip bulbs to a 6-inch container, depending on bulb size. Place the flat side of the tulip bulb against the side of the pot so that the lower limp leaf hangs over the edge of the pot.

Daffodils do best in a 3- to a 6-inch pot, with half the bulb showing above the soil.

Crocuses, snowdrops and grape hyacinths are planted one inch below the soil surface with an inch or two between plants.

After planting water each pot until the water runs out of the bottom.

Storage

The planted pots should now go into a cool area where the temperature does not go above 50°F. If you have a cool basement this may be the answer. Burying the pots outdoors is another suitable way to handle the crucial period. If you live in an apartment and don't have too many containers, the refrigerator will serve very well indeed. Keep fruits out of the refrigerator at this time because many of them release ethylene, a gas that can hasten flowering. Use the next to the bottom shelf to be sure the bulbs do not freeze. Water the soil as needed.

This picture shows several kinds of bulbs being forced and a variety of the types of containers that can be used.

Vermiculite (center) and pebbles (right) are two of the materials, or mediums, that may be used for forcing bulbs. Notice the manner in which the bulbs are placed in the pebbles in the bowl on the left.

The key to success here lies in getting the roots to develop without too much top development.

Forcing

The length of storage will never be less than ten weeks, and twelve weeks for large tulips, daffodils and iris.

When plants are removed from the refrigerator, yellow shoots should be showing. The plants should go into a partially shaded area with a temperature between 60°F. and 65°F. By all means avoid radiators, heat registers and warm rooms.

When the shoots begin to green up, gradually move the plants to brighter light intensity and a warmer temperature.

For a prolonged period of bloom, bulbs can be stored in and removed from the refrigerator at 2-4 week intervals.

Water culture

Hyacinths are often forced in water. Begin by buying a large bulb to assure a healthy bloom.

A French hyacinth glass jar can be bought readily. Place a bulb on the collar or rim and fill with water to ¼ inch from the bottom of the bulb. Be sure the water does not touch the bulb.

Some shops sell pre-stored hyacinth bulbs which can save you a waiting period. Be sure to check! If your bloom fails to appear, cover the glass container with an ordinary paper cup until the bloom begins to grow out.

Tender bulbs

Paperwhite narcissus

The yellow variety, Soleil d'Or, can be used as well as the white.

A shallow container 2 to 3 inches deep is suggested. It is filled to within ½ inch of the top with coarse sand, pebbles or gravel, and bulbs are set in the medium with their necks well exposed. Add

These bulbs are being placed in the pot with the flat side of each bulb facing toward the outside of the pot.

water to ½ inch below the surface of the medium.

Place the container in a well lighted location with a temperature of 60°F. or slightly below. Be sure the water level remains where it was at the start.

At a temperature of 60-70°F. blooming will begin in six weeks. To delay blooming, the pot can be held at 50°F. and then moved to a higher temperature.

After flowering the bulbs can be thrown out, or reused. If you want to try to force the bulbs again, store them out of the container at about 45-50°F. for twelve to fourteen weeks. They can then be repotted and placed at 60°F. in bright light. Within four to five weeks you will have more blooms.

Hardy bulbs

Amaryllis

Amaryllis is planted one bulb to a pot, with an inch of space around the bulb and half of the bulb above the soil line. Soil mix No. 2 is used.

Water well and set in a sunny location at a temperature of 60°F. or above. Flowering will begin six to eight weeks later. Keep watering the plants during this period of blooming.

After the flowers fade, cut the flower stalk off, continue watering, do some modest fertilizing and keep the plant in bright light.

When the danger of frost damage is past you can place the plants outdoors if you have a spot or they can be kept indoors. Late in August when the leaves begin to turn brown, decrease watering. By this time the leaves are dead. Allow the medium to dry out, then store the bulb and pot at 40°F. to 45°F. In January repot the bulb and begin the forcing procedure again. Any newly developed little bulbs can either remain on the mother to help form a clump or can be removed with a part of the root. The little ones will bloom in two or three years.

This glass container is specifically designed for the forcing of hyacinth. Notice the well formed roots with very little shoot growth.

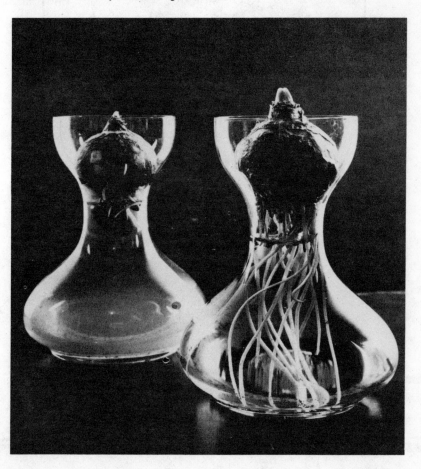

Bonsai

Bonsai are miniaturized trees and shrubs grown in pots, a technique we have imported from Japan. The basis for successful bonsai growing is the selection of those plants suited for indoor growth. Most bonsai require the out of doors most of the year and cannot be considered house plants. This is particularly true of forest trees. At the end of this chapter is a list adapted from the United States Department of Agriculture, of some tropical and sub-tropical plants particularly suited for indoor bonsai gardening.

There are several ways of getting started in bonsai. One is to buy suitable plants from local nurseries or specialty houses.

This Chinese elm was trained in the formal upright style.

Some indoor gardeners begin by collecting seed in the field, a bothersome process because seeds vary greatly in their germination requirements.

Others may collect small trees and plants in the wild, best done in the early spring before growth has begun. Such trees may be partially dwarfed already, due to the competition inherent in a wild plant ecosystem.

If you want to try your hand at collecting wild plants, collect plants in an area under development for building or roads, with permission of the developer, usually given willingly. In other cases, collecting of trees and shrubs must be approved by the landowner. Remember, no collecting can be done in national parks, national forests, state parks and state forests. Be sure the material you collect is not on your state's list of protected plants.

For outdoor collecting you will need the following equipment:

(1) large plastic freezer bags or plastic sheets for wrapping roots
(2) plastic bottle of water (which gets heavier as you climb)
(3) G.I. folding shovel for digging up plants
(4) peat moss, dampened if practical
(5) string to wrap plastic in place
(6) pruning shears to trim roots and branches
(7) trowel to dig up smaller plants

When you dig, try to leave a good ball of soil around the roots. Remember that the distribution of roots in the soil is about equal to the spread of the branches above ground. When removing a plant, cut about half the root away with the shovel or trowel. Handle the roots, and particularly the taproot (the principal root) if one is present, with great care. Harvest plants less than 2 feet in height. Trim off any damaged shoots or roots with the shears. Then pack handfuls of the dampened spagnum moss around the roots and wrap them in the plastic bags, or plastic sheet. Keep the leaves damp with water from the plastic bottle to minimize plant moisture loss.

At home, carefully remove the plastic and plant the tree in a pot slightly smaller than the roots seem to require. A media of 1/3 sand, 1/3 soil and 1/3 peat moss seems generally adaptable. Very carefully straighten the roots when planting to help later on in the shaping. As the trees mature in their containers, part of the upper roots may be

A mugho pine trained in the formal upright style.

is one. Also, a tree that tapers towards the top is considered suitable for bonsai. Exposure of roots has been mentioned before.

The plan

An aesthetically attractive bonsai tree should be planned for when you begin. The trunk-to-be should be visible to the lower third of the tree. The branches should be "balanced," not geometrically, but sufficiently to present a pleasing design. The top branches should be smaller than those below.

This gingko was trained in the informal upright style.

left exposed to give an old gnarled appearance.

Water the trees sparingly and use very little fertilizer if any. A year later, in the spring, move the tree carefully into a somewhat smaller container, trimming the roots back to about one half so as to enable the plant to fit. This procedure will be repeated once or twice more, repotting and pruning the roots by one half. At each repotting note carefully to see if the plants are pot-bound. The symptoms of this are the formation of a mat-like root growth. If this has happened, prune carefully to reduce by about one half.

Two or even three years after the plant has been collected it should be ready for the more technical bonsai training.

Plant qualities for bonsai use

There are two objective standards a tree should meet to serve as a sound bonsai. These are, small leaves or needles and a short distance between the point of origin of leaves.

There are also subjective requirements for a tree to qualify. A furrowed bark, or a bark that gives the impression of age even when very young,

126

Styles

There are five basic styles of bonsai, although all are subject to creative variations.

Formal upright. This is probably the simplest for the beginner. The form is conical or mildly rounded at the top and the branches are horizontal. Often, a lower branch extends a little further than the others. The two lowest branches may be trained to come forward slightly, with a third branch projecting at the back of the tree.

Informal upright style. This differs from the formal upright in that the main trunk slants slightly to one side. You can achieve this effect by potting a young tree at an angle.

Slanting style. The trunk slants much more than in the previous styles. The lowest branches should spread in the direction opposite to the trunk. The tree top may be slanted slightly towards the front.

Cascade style. The trunk begins to grow in an erect manner, then is trained down to reach a point below the bottom of the container. This style has the foliage growing below the soil surface. Low growing species are much easier to train than an erect tree.

Semi-cascade style. The change of growth direction is less abrupt than in the above. The foliage should not be allowed to grow below the bottom of the container.

Before selecting one of the five styles, study your specimen carefully to see which style will be most practical to develop.

Three operations are required to establish a finished bonsai: pruning, pinching and wiring.

Pruning

This is, by comparison to pinching, a large scale, major cutting out of unwanted foliage, and malformed and superfluous limbs. Remove crossing branches and dead branches and then carefully remove other branches until you begin to achieve the form you want.

A lodgepole pine trained in the slanting style.

This pyracantha, or firethorn, was trained in the cascade style.

Follow standard pruning procedures for sanitation, make pruning cuts above buds, and remove buds other than those on the outside of the tree.

Pinching

A relatively refined process of shaping a tree, used to remove new shoots before they become established. Pinching back new shoots will result in bushier growth. This can be done with the finger tips or a small sharp scissors. Any new or unwanted shoots or trunk and branches should be pinched back. Leave no stubs.

Pinching should accompany root pruning at repotting time, to maintain a balance between foliage and root system, and at other times as needed.

Wiring

This is the technique used to produce one of the final bonsai styles. Copper wires, sizes 10, 12, 14, 16 and 18 are commonly used, with 10 heavy and 18 light.

Deciduous plants are best wired during the spring and summer; evergreen plants during winter.

Begin the wiring at the bottom of the plant, pushing the end of the wire into the soil and working up. The wire used is wrapped loosely in a series of spirals about ¼ inch apart. A thin pad can be placed under the wire to protect the trunk from damage.

When wiring is complete, the trunk and main branches are gently bent in the desired direction. The wire helps keep the plant in position. If a branch snaps off, cut it back to the nearest side branch; if it is partly broken, fasten it in place with a small piece of rubber tape as it may heal.

At the end of the year remove the wire from the tree, using great care not to snap the foliage.

Plants used for indoor bonsai:

acacia, *Acacia baileyana*
aralia, *Polyscias balfouriana, P. fruticosa,*
    P. guilfoylei
Arizona cypress, *Cupressus arizonica*
boxwood, *Buxus sempervirens*
California pepper tree, *Schinus molle*
camellia, *Camellia japonica,* and *C. sasanqua*
Cape jasmine, *Gardenia jasminoides,*
    G. jasminoides radicans

Chinese pistachio, *Pistacia chinensis*
citrus, (calamondin, kumquat, lemon, lime,
    orange, and tangerine), *Citrus* spp.
classic myrtle, *Myrtus communis*
common olive, *Oleo europea*
cork oak, *Quercus suber*
dwarf pomegranate, *Punica granatum nana*
elfin herb, *Cuphea hypssopifolia*
hibiscus, *Hibiscus roseo-sinensis* Cooperi
Indian laurel, *Ficus retusa*
indoor oak, *Nicodemia diversifolia*
jacaranda, *Jacaranda acutifolia*
jade plant, *Crassula* spp.
jasmine, *Jasminum parkeri*
miniature holly, *Malpighia coccigera*
mistletoe fig, *Ficus diversifolia*
Montera cypress, *Cupressus macrocarpa*

A yellow star jasmine trained in the semi-cascade style.

Natal plum, *Carissa grandiflora*
orange jasmine, *Murraea exotica*
orchid tree, *Bauhinia variegata*
powderpuff tree, *Calliandra surinamensis*
pyracantha, *Pyracantha* spp.
royal poinciana, *Delonix regia*

shower tree, *Cassia eremophila*
silk oak, *Grevillea robusta*
star jasmine, *Trachelospermum jasminoides*
Surinam cherry, *Eugenia uniflora*
West Indian cherry, *Malpighia* spp.
white popinac, *Leucaena glauca*

Vegetable Growing in the Kitchen

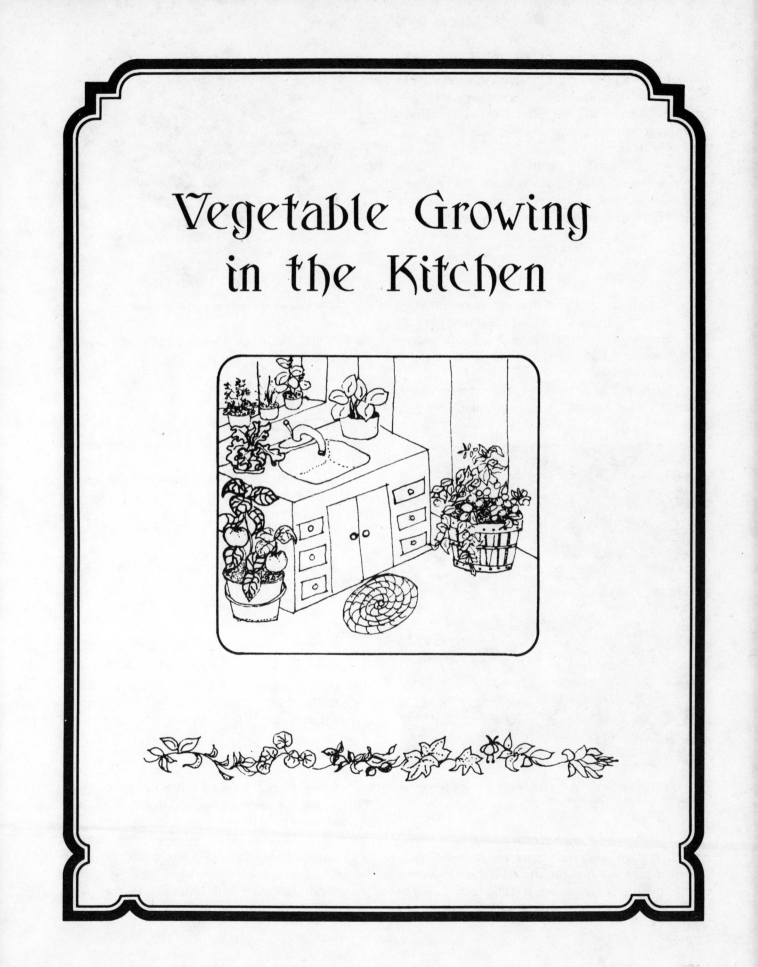

Odd as it may seem you can grow modest amounts of a pretty wide selection of vegetables in an apartment if you have a location which gets some sunlight: a window sill, a balcony, or a doorstep protected from dogs. Fire escapes are, by law, out of bounds.

All you need to be in the indoor vegetable business is a suitable container, seed and synthetic soil mixture. Plants vary greatly in their growth requirements and we have listed the special requirements of many.

Containers

Just about anything that allows for drainage will serve the purpose. You can use flower pots, an old pail, a simple plastic freezer bag, an old plastic dish, a wooden bushel basket lined with plastic or an old work bucket.

Be sure that you punch holes for drainage, usually 4 to 6¼ inches in diameter, along the bottom side.

White radishes can be grown in a plastic pail. Drainage is provided by punching holes in the side of the pail.

The container you select as well as how many, will depend on how much space you have available. Six-inch pots are fine for chives. Radishes, onions and miniature tomatoes are suitable for growing in 10- to 12-inch pots. Large 5 gallon plastic con-

Leaf lettuce will grow happily in a simple plastic bag.

tainers are fine if you have a space large enough to hold them.

Growth medium

The best soil substitute can be made by mixing this formula. It can be cut in half if need be, or increased.

> ¾ cubic foot package of shredded peat moss
> equal quantity of vermiculite
> ½ cup ground limestone
> ¼ cup 20 percent superphosphate
> ½ cup 5-10-5

Add a little water and mix well. We use a garbage can with a tight fitting cover for this, to minimize inhaling the dust.

Seeds

Small packets are readily available in almost any grocery, garden store and discount store. The year stamped on the packet tells you in which year the seed were meant to be grown.

Light requirements

Some vegetables need more sun than others. This will influence the kind you plant. If you have limited space with sunlight you will need to specialize in those vegetables that yield with less sunlight.

Some vegetables can be grown entirely in the house, using supplementary light sources. In this group fall radishes, leaf lettuce and the dwarf "Tiny Tim" tomato.

This tomato plant is a variety called "Tiny Tim." It can also be grown in a plastic pail.

Leaf lettuce finds a home in a bushel basket lined with a plastic bag.

Planting date

If you are in the position of having some out of doors for this project, you will need to know the date of the last frost in the spring. This is only an average date which can fall earlier or later in a given year. The local office of the National Climatic Center of the U.S. Department of Commerce, or the county agricultural extension agent, can tell you this date for your locality. The average date of first fall frost helps decide varieties to select, as some take longer to yield a crop than others.

Planting

If you start your plants four to eight weeks be-

fore last frost they will be ready to move to the exposed area you have in mind. You can start the plants in small pots, or in the peat discs described in the chapter on propagation. About two or three weeks after seeding, the plants to go outside should be hardened; that is done by reducing water and putting the plants in a cooler spot.

If you have a small number of plants set in an open area, they can possibly be brought indoors if a late frost moves in.

Water your plants each time the soil surface feels dry to the touch but avoid too much water. As the plants and the weather turn warmer, more water will be required.

Keep weeds out by pulling them up by hand.

A pepper plant will produce, even when planted in a plain metal bucket.

If you see any insects or diseases, use the appropriate dust recommended by your garden shop.

Light adaptability of some vegetables

Partial shade
beets
cabbage
carrots
chives

leek
leaf lettuce (tolerates low temperatures)
onions, green
parsley
radishes

Full sunlight
eggplant
peppers
tomatoes

Plant Pests

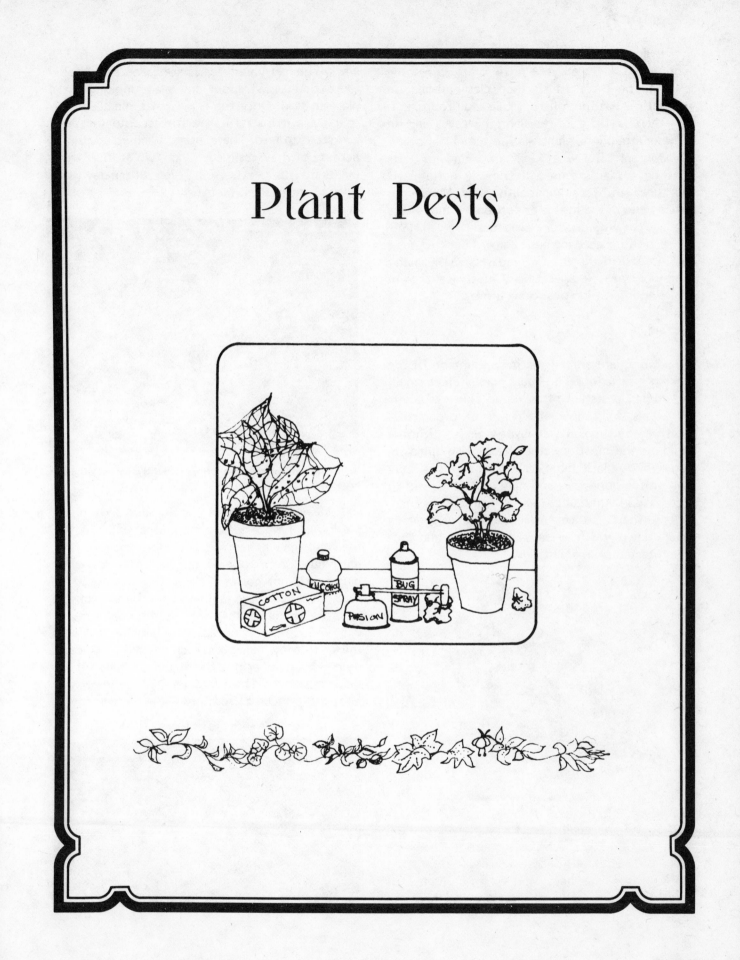

Even though you lavish fertilizer, proper lighting and water on your prize plants, something seems to be the matter! Upon closer inspection you notice that the foliage is pale and droops. Perhaps there is sticky substance on the leaves, and on the floor around the plant. As you turn a leaf over—egads, insects! But what kind? Two kinds of pests infest house plants, those with chewing mouth parts and those with sucking mouth parts. When you notice holes in the foliage or portions of the foliage missing, chewing pests are probably involved. (See the section on chewing pests below.) Sucking pests are more difficult to diagnose. However, many times honeydew, a sweet sticky substance, accompanies an infestation of sucking insects.

Sucking insects

Aphids are among the most common of the sucking insects found on house plants. These small, soft-bodied pests are often found clustered along the stems and under the leaves of ornamental plants. Many times the honeydew excreted by the aphids is the most noticeable part of an aphid infestation. A black mold, called sooty mold, may grow in the honeydew and may cause the plant to become dark and unattractive. Aphids are sometimes difficult to control because they tend to wedge down into the crevices of a plant and thus are protected from a pesticide.

Aphids feeding in a cluster.

Scales are small insects which are protected by a waxy or lacquer-like secretion. There are many different kinds of scales. Scales feed by sucking sap from the stems and leaves of their host plant. Female scales lay their eggs under their pro-tective cover, or scale, which protects the eggs. The newly hatched young scales are called crawlers because they crawl about the plant looking for a place to feed. Once the crawler has selected a suitable place it inserts its mouthpart into the plant and starts to feed. These insects are hard to control because of their scale covering. Two or three treatments may be necessary at seven- or ten-day intervals to control these pests.

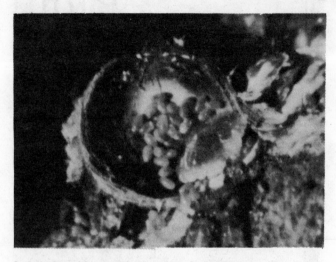

Scale insect with protective covering raised shows her body and eggs underneath.

Mealybugs are related to scales and aphids. Mealybugs have a soft, waxy bloom which covers their body giving them a mealy appearance. At first, mealybugs seem to hide on the plant and their presence is not noticed. Later, however, after the first mealybugs have laid eggs and the tiny mealybugs have hatched, the infestation becomes shockingly noticeable! The eggs are usually laid in a thick, cottony mass. As each female produces a prodigious number of offspring mealybugs are difficult to control. The eggs enmeshed in the cottony mass are protected from pesticides. Also many of

A mealy bug feeding on a coleus.

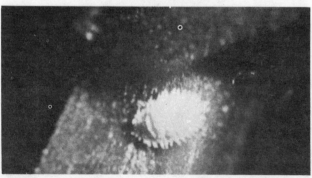

the individuals tend to wedge themselves into crevices on the plant and are untouched by the pesticide.

Whiteflies are those snow white, gnatlike insects which fly up from a plant when it is disturbed. Female whiteflies lay their eggs on the underside of the leaves. Tiny crawlers hatch from these eggs in a few days. The crawlers settle down and insert their mouth parts into the bottom of the leaf and begin feeding. It takes about three weeks for the whitefly larva to develop to a pupal stage. Whitefly adults emerge from the pupal stage within four or five days. The immature stages of the whitefly are very, very difficult to kill with ordinary pesticides. (However, house plant pesticides which contain pyrethrin, a plant product, are effective against the immature stages of whiteflies.) Like aphids, scale and mealybugs, whiteflies excrete honeydew. Plants may become covered with the sticky substance. Sooty mold may also grow in the honeydew and ruin the appearance of the plant.

Whitefly adults gather on the under side of a leaf of their host plant.

Thrips are small and slender, but they are not particularly cute. The blooms of white or light-colored flowers are often infested with thrips in the summer. Thrips wedge their way into the buds and feed on the petals with their rasping, sucking mouth parts before the blossoms open. After opening, the petals may appear brownish, distorted and unattractive. Thrips are not resistant to most pesticides but their small size makes them easily over-

looked and often the damage is done before their presence is noticed.

Spider mites are not really insects but are more closely related to spiders. They suck out the contents of their host plant cells on the lower portion of the leaf causing tiny spots to appear on the leaves. Many times a thin web is noticed on the plant; hence the name spider mite. Spider mites lay their eggs on the leaves and stems of their host plant. Within a few days, tiny larvae hatch from the eggs and begin to feed. Between each stage is a form called the resting stage or nymphochrysalis. The eggs and resting stages are exceedingly tolerant to pesticides. Therefore, when you treat for spider mites, repeat the pesticide application in seven days and perhaps follow up with a third application in another seven to ten days. Spider mites are small but they are visible with outstretched legs; an adult would approximately cover the period at the end of this sentence.

Spider mite damage to a potted palm.

Spider mites and their eggs. Note the loose webbing.

137

Cyclamen mites are much smaller than spider mites and are completely invisible to the unaided human eye. Their small size allows them to burrow into crevices and buds of house plants and to feed there long before the buds open. Their feeding causes tremendous distortion and the eventual death of the plant. Cyclamen mites are exceptionally sensitive to heat however and one may rid small plants of cyclamen mites by submerging the plant for fifteen minutes in water which has been heated to 110°F. Like spider mites, cyclamen mites lay eggs; however, there is only one immature stage, the larval. Cyclamen mites are fragile and, as mentioned before, sensitive to heat. However, because they burrow into the buds and crevices of a plant they are many times almost inaccessible to pesticides. A presticide must be applied very, very thoroughly to rid a plant of these pests.

Chewing insects

Caterpillars are the immature stages of moths and butterflies. Butterflies and moths usually lay their eggs directly on the host plant. The newly hatched caterpillars first eat their egg shell and then venture out on the plant, feeding upon the foliage or boring into the stem. Caterpillars are usually not a pest of house plants unless they are kept on an open porch or patio. Some caterpillars web the foliage together and hide within the webbed mass. Other caterpillars feed openly on the plant and can therefore be easily controlled either by picking off or spraying.

Grasshoppers are occasionally a pest of house

The scalloped appearance of grasshopper damage.

plants if the windows are left open or plants are kept on an open porch. Adult grasshoppers fly onto the plant and feed on the edges of the foliage so that the foliage has a characteristic notched appearance. Grasshoppers are not difficult to control because they are large and conspicuous. They can easily be picked off or sprayed with a house plant pesticide.

Leaf miners, the immature stages of flies and moths, are among the most difficult plant pests to control. The most common leaf miner pests of indoor house plants are leaf miner flies. The female flies deposit their eggs in the surface of the leaves and the young larval begins to feed on the tissue between the surfaces of the leaf. Feeding by the larvae makes a conspicuous visible tunnel which detracts from the appearance of the leaf. If the infestation is heavy enough, the plant will be damaged by the excessive number of tunnels. When treating for leaf miner pests of indoor house plants, be sure and carry the plant outdoors when you spray it and allow the plant to remain outdoors until it is thoroughly dry.

The marbilization caused by leaf miner damage.

Fungus gnats are an occasional pest on indoor house plants. The adult flies look like miniature mosquitoes with dark wings and no beak. The flies lay their eggs on the soil of house plants, and the tiny maggots begin feeding on the root hairs of the plants. As the maggots mature, they consume more and more roots. Finally, they work their way up the inside of the main stem of the plant, com-

APHIDS

Soft-bodied, sucking insects clustering on stems, in crevices, and under leaves of ornamental plants. Secrete honeydew which may grow a sooty mold. Cause stunted and distorted plant growth. Dip in or spray thoroughly with insecticide.

CYCLAMEN MITES

Invisible to naked eye. Oval, almost transparent pests that burrow into young leaves and buds causing deformation. Isolate infested plant. Remove affected portions of the plant if possible. Dip in or spray with pesticide. Very thorough application is required.

MEALYBUGS

Sucking, soft-bodied, powdery-appearing insects. Secrete honeydew which may grow black mold. Eggs are laid in a cotton-like web that protects them from pesticides. Dab pests with cotton soaked in alcohol. Or, dip in or pressure-spray with insecticide.

SCALES

Small insects protected by a waxy shell-like secretion. May infest stems and leaves, sucking the sap and causing stunted growth. Also secrete honeydew. Dip in or spray with insecticide. Several thorough applications may be necessary in order to penetrate the protective shell.

SPIDER MITES

Visible only in clusters. Usually red in color. Prefer undersides of leaves. Infected plants become stunted; leaves may yellow and drop. Spray with or dip in pesticide, especially the leaf undersides. Repeat at weekly intervals to destroy newly hatched individuals.

THRIPS

Barely visible tan, brown, or black winged insects. Feed on plant juices causing distortion. Common during the summer months, especially on plants with white or light-colored blooms. Dip in or spray with insecticide.

WHITEFLIES

White, flying insects which thrive on plant juices. Suck at leaf bases, draining them of their color. Secrete honeydew which may develop black mold. Spray with or dip in insecticide. Several treatments may be necessary.

pletely destroying it. Fungus gnat larvae pupate in the soil and soon new flies emerge to begin laying eggs around other plants.

When *snails* and *slugs* are found on indoor house plant pests, they have usually been carried in on the pot. Snails and slugs use their peculiar rasp-like tongues to chew holes in the plant foliage. Females lay eggs. Soon, tiny slugs are merrily chewing away at your plant. Inspect the sides and bottom of any pots that are brought into the house to prevent infestation of snails and slugs. Disgustingly enough, hand picking is probably the best control.

Plant-associated pests

A number of indoor pests do not feed upon the plants themselves but are merely associated with the plants.

Ants, although arduous, are awfully aggravating. Ants usually do not feed upon ornamental plants; however, their small mounds can be a nuisance and the fact that they many times feed on food which has been left out in the kitchen make ants an indoor pest. Because the nests of ants are sometimes found in house plants it is necessary to treat the soil of the house plant in order to control the ants.

Psocids are also called *barklice* and *booklice.* Psocids feed on a variety of dead organic matter but almost never on ornamental plants. Because psocids at times become numerous on the soil and pots of house plants, you may become alarmed at their presence.

Sowbugs and *pillbugs* are often found around the bases of ornamental plants left on a porch or patio. At times sowbugs and pillbugs will feed on ornamental plants, but most of the time they merely feed on decaying organic matter and are therefore harmless. These can be swept or vacuumed up and eliminated quickly. However, if a pesticide is applied it should be applied around the outside of the house in order to eliminate the sowbugs and pillbugs at their source rather than inside the house.

Control of house plant pests

Now that you know everything there is to know about house plant pests, controlling these pests is the only thing left to learn. Preventive, mechanical and chemical methods of control are names for doing-in these beasties inhabiting your plant growth.

Preventive control involves carefully inspecting every plant for pests before you buy it or bring it into the vicinity of your other prized plant possessions. Never buy a plant which is infested with any of the vicious pests for such plants will bring you grief! Preventing an infestation is much cheaper and easier than eliminating pests firmly entrenched on your plants!

Mechanical control is a cheap, although time-consuming, method of eliminating pests. Hand picking or wiping the pests off must be done thoroughly. A cotton swab dipped in alcohol or fingernail polish remover is an effective tool for eliminating mealybugs, scales and aphids. Washing plants with a soft brush and gentle detergent will remove sooty mold and aphids, spider mites and mealybugs. If the plants are sturdy enough, a stream of water will knock most of the insects and spider mites from the plants. However, always keep an eye on the plants in case of reinfestation.

Chemical control is a gratifying method of murdering those pests. Just spray a pesticide on and watch them fall off. However, pesticides can be dangerous when misused. A few common sense rules should be followed for safe application:

1. Always store pesticides away from food or feed and under lock and key.

2. Do not let children or careless persons handle pesticide containers or apply pesticides.

3. Whenever possible, carry your plants outdoors to apply the pesticide. Wait until the plant is dry before returning it to the house (it is safe to handle the plants after the pesticides mentioned below have dried).

4. Don't mix excessive amounts of pesticides. What little pesticide that is left over after treatment can be poured down the toilet.

5. Always follow the directions for safe use found on the label of whatever pesticide is used.

Malathion will control most sucking insects. You may have to use a small amount of household detergent to make the mixture spread properly on plants with waxy leaves (about ½ teaspoon per gallon of water). *Malathion* is sold as a dust, wettable powder or liquid. The 50 to 57 percent liquid is most suitable for use on house plants. Mix ½ teaspoon of *malathion* in one quart of water with a dash of detergent to make the correct concentration. This mixture can be sprayed on the plant or the plant can be dipped into the mixture. Remember! For good control, thorough application is essential. Even so, several applications of *malathion* may be necessary for whitefiles and mealybugs.

Sevin is a very good pesticide for control of chewing insects. *Sevin* comes formulated in so many concentrations that the least confusing thing to say is mix *Sevin* according to the directions on the label. *Sevin* will not control slugs, however. Use a prepared bait or mixture containing *metaldehyde* for slugs. The pot and bait should be placed out of the reach of pets and children, outdoors if possible.

Pyrethrins, a plant product, give a quick knock-down of insects. *Pyrethrins* are very safe to use and are very short lived in the environment. You may want to use a *pyrethrin aerosol* because of its safety and convenience. *Pyrethrins* are generally effective for whitefly. However, several applications at four or five day intervals may be necessary for complete control of whiteflies.

Chlordane is the pesticide to use for soil inhabiting insect pests. *Chlordane* is long lasting in the soil so that one good application is usually enough. *Chlordane* is usually formulated as a percent mixture and is mixed at a rate of 1½ teaspoons per quart.

A word of caution: *Use only pesticides labeled for application on plants. Many pesticides for flying and crawling insects are formulated with a refined kerosene solvent. This kerosene will kill your plants!*

Malathion, Sevin, metaldehyde, pyrethrins and *chlordane* are all available at hardware stores, retail nurseries and garden shops and centers. Although it is cheaper per unit of volume to buy pesticides in the larger bottles, many times it is better to purchase the smallest package available. There are several reasons: In case of a broken bottle, the less pesticide spilled the better. Unless you have a tremendous number of infested house plants you will be surprised at how long a bottle of pesticide will last you. And pesticides do age with time; some lose their effectiveness in controling pests, and some may become more likely to clog your sprayer or to damage your plants.

Now the only thing left to do is to get up, grab your sprayer and kill those pests!

Plant Diseases

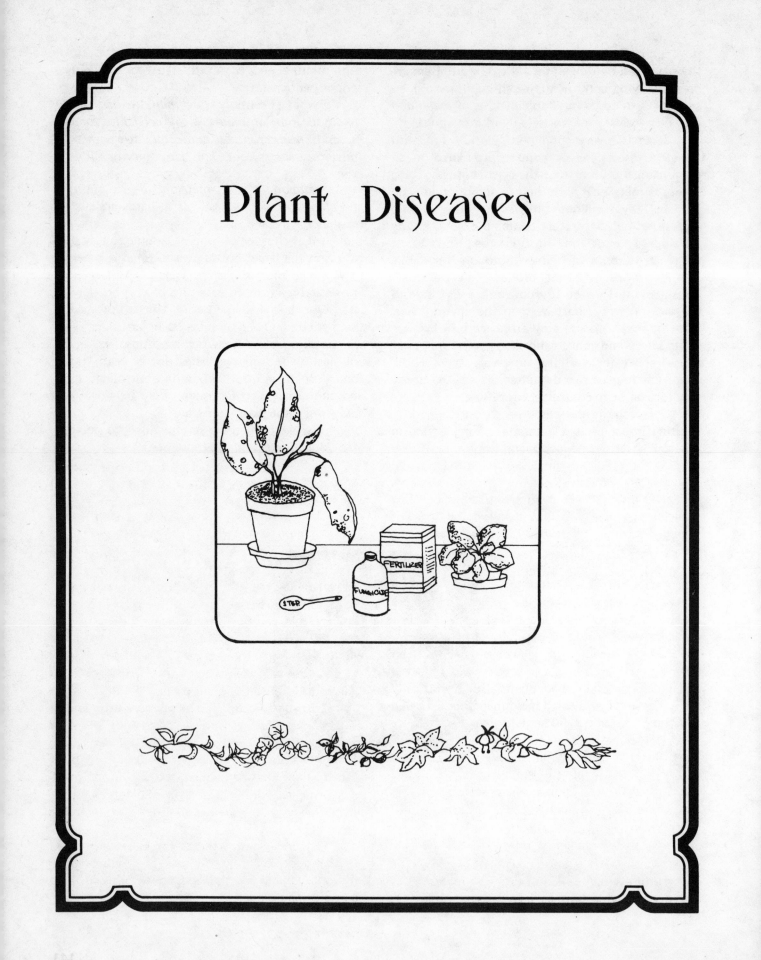

Though house plants are as susceptible to disease as garden plants, they are seldom infected because of cleanliness and sanitation practices followed by the indoor gardener that are impossible to apply outdoors. Likewise, house plants are rarely damaged by environmental conditions because they are sheltered from snow, wind, sleet, hail and other potentially damaging elements. Gardeners find that it's much easier to protect plants from disease than it is to care for them, so let's discuss what precautions you can take to protect your plants from disease, and yourself from the work, expense and trouble of replacing sick specimens.

To help guard against disease and disease-causing factors it is useful to know a few basic biological facts. We should all become familiar with just what disease is. Very simply, disease is any condition that is not normal. Changes in the physical appearance of plants, such as leaf yellowing or browning, are keys to such situations and are called "symptoms." The occurrence of such symptoms can be caused by biotic or living factors, as well as by abiotic or non-living factors. A biotic factor may be a fungus, virus, bacterium or nematode. Abiotic factors would include such things as too much water, not enough fertilizer, cold and so on. The remainder of this chapter will be devoted to guidelines pointing out how to prevent and, if necessary, treat the occurrence of biotic and abiotic disease-causing agents.

First is careful shopping. Always buy your house plants from a reliable dealer, one that will replace any diseased specimens free of charge. Also remember that plants bought from casual sources are sometimes inexpensive but may harbor disease-causing organisms that could not only destroy your recently purchased plants but also could spread to and kill more established plants. But if you can't resist a sale, carry a small hand magnifier with you (purchased for about 50 cents) to get a really close look at the merchandise. Look for any growth or markings that are not the same or characteristic coloring as the plant (this could be fungal or bacterial growth). Of course, many organisms that may prove harmful may still escape detection but make the effort anyway. Ask the salesperson about anything on the plant that does not seem normal. Once you've carried your new plants home, keep a watchful eye on them. Inspect them regularly for any disease symptoms as given in the following paragraphs. Treat the purchase and care of a house plant with the same concern and care you might give a new kitten, puppy or any other living thing.

Second, always do your best to keep potting materials and tools free of disease-causing organisms (in other words, "biotic" agents collectively known as "pathogens"). It is a good practice, if time allows, to dust and repot all new arrivals. Leaves should be dusted as often as your furniture, once or twice a month. Dust reduces the amount of needed light that reaches the leaf surface and can also trap disease-causing spores. Leaves can be washed with a mild solution of soapy water and a soft cloth. (Some house plant lovers swear by skim milk, saying that it leaves a brighter shine.) A few gentle strokes remove dust which might carry disease spores and the leaves of your house plant will really shine! Fuzzy-leaved plants, like African violets, can be dusted lightly with a camel's hair brush, one of those brushes made especially for infants. Avoid artificial shiners in aerosol cans because there is a great possibility of damage if they are used incorrectly. Soap and water leaves all the shine you could possibly desire. Dracaenas, especially, benefit from a good bath once every month as do most glossy-leaved plants.

Third, if you put your house plants outside for the summer, spray them with a general garden disinfectant (fungicide, bacteriacide) *before bringing them in for the winter.* It is quite possible that organisms which remain low in number while exposed to outdoor weather conditions might undergo a population boom once they are moved into a comfortable, warm, relatively humid home.

Fourth, remove diseased leaves, stems, and flowers as soon as they appear. Dying plant material can support the speedy growth of pathogens that can spread to healthy plant parts.

Last, be sure to keep plants as healthy as possible through *proper watering, fertilizing and light and temperature regulation.* Most house plant problems are a result of improper watering and over-fertilization. Just as people are more prone to illness when run down, so are house plants. A strong plant is less likely to become diseased than is a weak plant.

Of course, house plants can become diseased regardless of conscientious care. The following listings should help you to diagnose and, hopefully, to cure sick house plants.

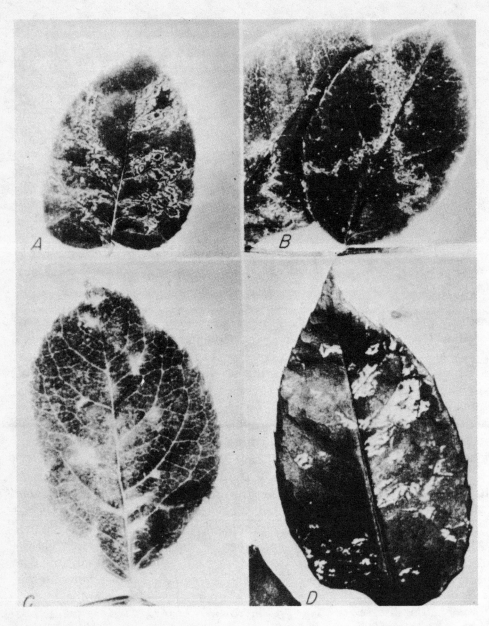

Virus diseases are difficult to identify and impossible to treat. If you are able to diagnose your plant's ailment as a viral infection, destroy it immediately. These photographs show rose leaflets suffering from a virus disease known as rose mosaic.

Please *be sure to carefully follow directions on the containers* of all chemicals used. The misuse of these compounds can sometimes cause you to experience very uncomfortable and unpleasant side effects.

There are quite a few problems and symptoms that can appear on just about any house plant. These signs are usually caused by the same abiotic or biotic agents regardless of what type of plant is affected.

Wilting is commonly caused by improper watering (too much or too little) or by the excessive use of fertilizer.

Rx: vary your watering schedule. Wait until the soil is "bone" dry before watering. It helps to poke your finger into the soil for about an inch to make certain that it's not just the surface soil that's dry.

Loss of Leaves. Sudden changes in temperature, lighting and/or ventilation could produce such symptoms. Unburned gas fumes can elicit such results from house plants.
Rx: try moving the plant to a different part of the room or to a different room entirely.

Yellowing and Death of Lower Leaves. This can be seen especially on woody house plants such

as dracaenas, rubber plants, palms, etc. Too little nitrogen or root crowding could be the culprit here.
Rx: try feeding your plant a fertilizer containing nitrogen and/or transfer to a larger pot.

Overall Yellowing of Leaves. Soil moisture is usually too high in this instance. It's possible that this condition has already caused the roots of your plant to rot.
Rx: repot this plant, making sure that drainage is adequate. Reduce watering.

Leaves Look Small and Stunted. Open those curtains! Too little light most often induces this condition.
Rx: increase the amount of light available to this plant.

Brown Corky Scab on Undersides of Leaves. This symptom is most often seen in late winter. (Geraniums are especially susceptible.) Overwatering and/or improper ventilation are possible villains.
Rx: reduce watering and provide better ventilation.

Browning Tips of Leaves. This problem is common with larger plants! The cause (or causes) is a difficult one to single out. Excess fertilizer, hot dry air and/or improper watering have been known to produce such symptoms.
Rx: experimentation and close observation are the treatments here. Move the plant around trying different locations while varying your watering habits. Good luck! You'll need it to unravel this problem!

Brown Spots, Yellow Margins and/or Tips On Leaves. African violets are especially vulnerable! Too much light affects most house plants this way.
Rx: reduce the amount of light or the intensity of light (i.e., move the plant from a southern to a western or northern exposure). Be especially wary and observant during late spring and summer.

White, Powdery Growth On Leaves, Buds, and Stems. What you're seeing here is the growth of a fungus. This problem is commonly referred to as "mildew." Sound familiar? The same thing can happen to your shower curtains or damp clothes. The cause of its appearance is the same in all instances: too much moisture.
Rx: keep your plant foliage dry. You can try spraying with *Karathane* or *Benlate* (follow the directions printed on the container).

Death of Seedlings. This occurs quite often and is usually accompanied by a dark rot on the seedling stem at soil level. One or many fungi can cause this.
Rx: the best thing to do here is to discard all seedlings and start over. Next time pay closer attention to your sterilization procedure.

Just about all of the symptoms mentioned above and in the rest of this chapter can also be induced by pathogenic microorganisms as well as by abiotic factors. Since these organisms, i.e., viruses, bacteria, fungi and nematodes, are not easily seen it would be practically impossible for you to detect their presence before their damage to your house plants is visible. If all of the suggested treatments fail to cure the plant, it is quite possible that a biotic agent is present. In this instance discard the diseased specimen and begin again, paying special attention to sterilization and potting procedures.

Certain diseases exist to which only specific indoor plants are susceptible. The following table is a general, though not by any means complete, listing of the symptoms and treatments for these damaging relationships.

PLANT	SYMPTOMS	TREATMENT
African violet	—bleached or tan spots leaves —leaves are crinkled and have a mosaic pattern of light and dark green areas	—keep foliage dry —discard sick plants

	—tan-colored fuzz and rot also appears on buds flowers and leaves	—provide better ventilation —keep foliage dry —spray with *Captan* (1½ tsp. to a quart of water)
	—black, slimy rot can affect stem, roots or crown of plants	—reduce watering —discard infected plants —sterilize soil and container before reusing
asparagus fern	—leaves turn brown, winter and fall	—lower room temperature, 70-72°F.
begonia	—large, round swellings on stem —tan-colored fuzz and rot	—discard infected plants (see African violets)
cactus	—corky, rust-colored spots, plants may fail to flower	—increase light —decrease humidity
caladium	—soft, mushy rotting tuber	—discard infected bulbs and check to be sure new bulbs are healthy (reputable businesses will guarantee their plant material)
English ivy	—spots on stems are mushy and light green. Spots turn brown or black with a red margin.	—water plants from below
fern	—swollen areas or knots on leaves	—galls are not a sign of disease but are a natural part of this plant
gardenia	—discolored, sunken areas on stem at soil level. Leaves wilt, yellow and fall. —bleached, yellow leaves with green veins. Entire plant looks weak. —buds fall from plants before opening	—reduce water and improve drainage —treat with *Sequestrene* (follow directions on label) —raise temperature and avoid sudden temperature changes —keep humidity high
geranium	—discolored areas or spots appear on leaves of plant —black, slimy rot on leaves etc.	—pick off and destroy affected leaves —see African violet
peperomia	—light, green rings appear on leaves —plants are stunted and distorted —black, slimy rot on leaves etc.	—repot —discard infected plants —see African violet

philodendron (also affects Chinese evergreen, dumb cane)	—dead regions on leaves —leaves have brown spots	—avoid too low temperatures —keep foliage dry —spray with *Zineb*
poinsettia	—leaves turn yellow and fall —black, slimy rot etc.	—refer also to general diseases —expose to warmer temperature —increase light —see African violet
rubber plant	—bleached or tan spots on leaves —spots of dead tissue will dry up and fall out	—move to lower light intensity —increase humidity —spray with *Zineb* (1½ tsp. to a quart of water)

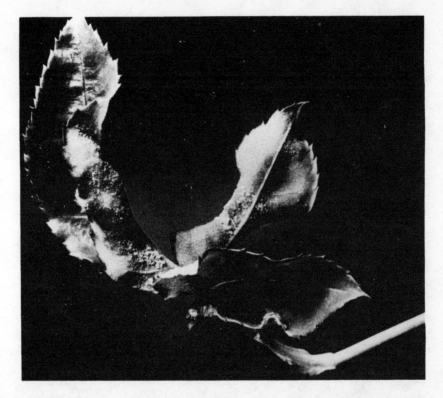

Mildews are common on all kinds of plants. Usually, powdery white masses appear on young shoots, leaves and buds. Distortion of the leaves is also visible in this photograph.

Hobby Greenhouses

A hobby greenhouse can range from a simple polyethylene covered framework that you can put together in an afternoon for less than seventy-five dollars to a six-thousand dollar fully automated conservatory.

No matter which size or type of greenhouse you choose, consider how much time you'll have to spend in it after it's built. Don't be over enthusiastic; some new greenhouse owners find they do not have as much time as they thought for gardening. On the other hand, there is a misconception that greenhouses require constant attention. By combining automatic controls and easy-care plants, maintenance can be kept to an hour a week. Automatic controls are ideal for providing proper growing temperature, artificial light, watering, humidity, and ventilation. If you have time, however, you can save a lot of money by not using automatic controls.

You can get the most greenhouse for your money by doing some of the construction work yourself.

TYPES OF GREENHOUSES

There are two basic types of greenhouses: attached and free standing. An attached greenhouse may be even-span, lean-to, or window-mounted. A freestanding greenhouse is usually even-span (symmetrical roof).

Attached lean-to

A lean-to greenhouse is built against a building, using the existing structure for one or more of its sides.

The lean-to is limited to single or double-row plant benches with a total width of seven to 12 feet. It can be as long as the building it is attached to. The advantage of the lean-to greenhouse is that it usually is close to available electricity, water, and heat.

The lean-to has the disadvantage of offering limited space, light, ventilation and temperature control.

Attached even-span

The even-span greenhouse is similar to a free-standing structure except that it is attached to a

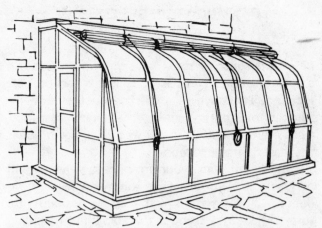

This glass-to-ground even span can be built free-standing or attached, as shown. This "all glass" model accommodates 3 full-size benches plus shelves.

house at one gable end. It can accommodate two or three rows of plant benches.

The cost of an even-span greenhouse is greater than the cost of a lean-to type, but it has greater flexibility in design and provides for more plants.

Because of its size and greater amount of exposed glass area, the even-span greenhouse will cost more to heat.

Attached window-mounted

A window-mounted greenhouse will allow space to grow a few plants at relatively low cost for heating and cooling. This reach-in greenhouse is available in many standard sizes, either in single units or in tandem arrangements for large windows. Only simple tools are needed to remove the regular window from the frame and fasten the prefabricated window greenhouse in its place.

Free-standing

The free-standing greenhouse is a separate structure and consists of side walls, end walls, and gable roof. It is like an even-span except that a free-standing greenhouse is set apart from other buildings to get the most sun. It can be made as large or small as desired.

A separate heating system is necessary unless the greenhouse is very close to a heated building. The free-standing greenhouse is more easily adapted to the builder's ideas of location, size, and shape than attached greenhouses. It also provides more light, but requires more heat at night due to the additional glass.

LOCATING YOUR GREENHOUSE

The first choice for a greenhouse site should be on the south or southeast side of the house in a sunny location. The east side is the second best location. That's where it will capture the most November to February sunlight. The next best locations are the southwest and west. The north side is the least desirable location.

You can place your greenhouse where it will be partly shaded during the summer when light reduction is not serious and may be desirable. Be sure to take into account the possibility of falling limbs that can damage the greenhouse.

Sometimes you can place a greenhouse against a door, window, or basement entrance of your house. This will let you use heat from your house to grow plants, make your greenhouse more accessible, and save on construction costs. Your home heating bill, however, will increase significantly.

If you have an L-shaped house, you can save the cost of two greenhouse walls by building the greenhouse in the "L".

Whether your greenhouse runs north and south or east and west is not as important as wind protection. Protect your greenhouse from winds by locating it so existing buildings will shield it, or by providing it with a windbreak hedge or fence.

DESIGNING YOUR GREENHOUSE

Width is the most important dimension; it will not be changed during the life of the greenhouse. Length can be increased if more space is desired.

Greenhouse width

Determine the width of your greenhouse by adding the widths of the plant benches and the walks. Allow approximately six inches for walls at either side and two inches for an air-circulation space between the side walls and the benches.

Side benches are serviced from only one side and should be no wider than you can reach across.

Center benches are serviced from both sides and can be as wide as six feet.

Determine the width of the walks in your greenhouse by how they are to be used. If the walks will be used only as a place to stand while servicing the benches, an 18- or 19-inch walk is suf-

ficiently wide; if a wheelbarrow will be brought into the greenhouse, the width must be greater.

Greenhouse length

Determine the length of your greenhouse by multiplying the number of plants you can grow across the benches by the number of plants you want to grow. Then round off the measurement so that no glass will need to be cut to fill odd sash bar spacings. (A sash bar is a shaped wooden or metal

This lean-to is 10 feet wide and allows enough room for two 36-inch wide benches along each wall. Glass shelves and hanging baskets may also be installed.

bar used in the construction of a sash or frame and designed to hold and support the glass securely to it.)

Standard glass sizes are 16 by 24, 18 by 20, and 20 by 20 inches. A larger glass size means fewer sash bars and less shadow inside the greenhouse. Most plastics are available in 100-foot lengths.

When you figure the length of a glass greenhouse, allow for the width of the projecting part of each sash bar plus a fraction of an inch clearance. For plastic, allow an extra 24 inches to fasten the plastic properly.

Greenhouse height

The height of the greenhouse depends on the desired height to the eave. An eave height of five feet is satisfactory for side benches with low-growing plants. If you want to grow tall plants, however, you will want an eave height of six or seven feet.

The pitch of the roof should be six in 12 (approximately 27 degrees). The eave height, the distance from the side wall to the center of the greenhouse, and the roof pitch will determine the height of your greenhouse at the center.

The height of the greenhouse should be equal to the eave height plus one-fourth the width of the greenhouse.

For instance, in an even-span greenhouse 18 feet wide, the distance from the side wall to the center of the greenhouse is nine feet. The difference in height between the center of the greenhouse and the eave will be one-half of nine feet, or four-and-one-half feet. If the eave is five feet high, the greenhouse should be nine-and-one-half feet at the center.

TYPES OF CONSTRUCTIONS

Greenhouses have supporting framework made of wood, aluminum, iron, or galvanized pipe. Some have curved eaves; others have flat eaves. Some are glass or plastic from the ground up. All types have advantages and disadvantages.

If you build your own greenhouse, have the plumbing and electrical work done by professionals in accordance with local codes. Most local governments require a building permit to erect a greenhouse.

Glass greenhouse

Glass is the traditional greenhouse covering. It is available in many designs to blend with almost any style of architecture. Glass greenhouses may have slanted sides, straight sides and eaves, or curved eaves.

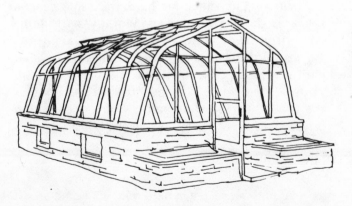

A free-standing greenhouse is set apart from other buildings. The door is located in one end. Very long units have a door at each end.

Aluminum, maintenance-free glass construction has very pleasing lines and will provide a large growing area. It assures you of a weather-tight structure, which minimizes heat costs and retains humidity.

For amateur gardeners, small prefabricated glass greenhouses are availalbe for do-it-yourself installation. They are sold in different models, to fit both available space and your pocketbook.

The disadvantages of glass are that it is easily broken, expensive, and requires a much better type of construction than fiberglass and plastic.

Fiberglass greenhouses

Fiberglass is lightweight, strong, and practically hailproof. Corrugated panels eight to 12-feet long and flat fiberglass in rolls are available in 24- to 48-inch widths. Thicknesses range from 3/64 to 3/32 of an inch.

Poor grades of fiberglass will discolor and the discoloring reduces light penetration. Using a good grade, on the other hand, may make your fiberglass greenhouse as expensive to build as a glass one. If you select fiberglass, choose the clearest grade.

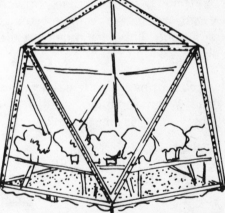

Greenhouses come in a number of types, styles and sizes. For the handyman, a plastic tri-penta greenhouse can provide do-it-yourself satisfaction.

Plastic greenhouses

Plastic greenhouses are increasing in popularity. The reasons are:

Construction cost per square foot is generally one-sixth to one-tenth the cost of glass greenhouses.

Plastic greenhouses can be heated as satisfactorily as glass greenhouses.

Crops grown under plastic are of equal quality to those grown under glass.

Polyethylene

The advantages of polyethylene are that it is low in cost and lightweight. It also stands up well in fall, winter and spring weather, and lets through plenty of light for good plant growth. However, polyethylene constantly exposed to the sun deteriorates during the summer and must be replaced each year.

Ultraviolet light energy causes polyethylene to break down. Ultraviolet-inhibited polyethylene lasts longer than regular polyethylene and is available in two- and six-mil thicknesses up to 40 feet wide and 100 feet long.

Polyethylene permits passage of much of the reradiated heat energy given off by the soil and plants inside the greenhouse. Therefore, a polyethylene greenhouse loses heat more quickly than a glass greenhouse both during sunny periods and after sunset. This is an advantage during the day and a disadvantage at night.

Polyvinyl chloride (PVC or Vinyl)

Vinyls from three to 12 mils thick are available for greenhouse covering. Like polyethylene, vinyls are soft and pliable; some are transparent, others translucent. They are usually available in four- to six-foot widths only; larger widths can be made.

Vinyls cost from two to five times as much as polyethylene. When carefully installed, 8- or 12-mil vinyl holds up for as long as five years.

TYPES OF FRAMES

If you plan to build a plastic greenhouse, careful consideration should be given to economy of size and future expansion.

Because plastic is available in large widths and is lighter in weight, greenhouse rafters and supporting members can be widely spaced to permit maximum light penetration. Common types of greenhouse frames are as follows.

A-Frame

In building an A-frame structure, consideration must be given to the placement of cross rafters (supporting members). Cross rafters should be placed at least one-third of the distance down from the ridge on the outer rafters. Otherwise, it will be difficult to work around the cross rafters in applying an insulating layer of plastic.

When the cross-rafter support is high in the peak of the greenhouse—especially in narrow greenhouses—an essentially clear-span type of structure permits easy application of an inner layer of plastic. The inner layer can be applied under the cross-rafter supports, leaving a small triangular air space in the peak of the house.

Diagonal bracing wires provide added strength to an A-frame structure.

Rigid Frame

Rigid-frame structures have been designed in widths up to 40 feet. This clear span structure has no columns to hold up the roof section.

The best available rigid-frame greenhouse has a six-foot sidewall and is designed for 30, 36, or 40-foot widths.

Panel Frame

Panel-frame greenhouses are a modification of the sash house (a small plastic greenhouse used for growing plants for later transplanting). This structure requires accurate carpentry, and construction costs are higher than for other frames.

Advantages of panels are that they can be quickly installed and taken down and stored during the summer; this will increase the life of the plastic.

Quonset

Quonset greenhouses have the same general shape as the quonset huts of World War II. Some have been constructed of wood, but usually the frames are metal. The half-circle frames are covered with one piece of wide plastic and the houses are up to 20 feet wide. The advantage of this house is the ease of construction and covering. Ventilation is by exhaust fans at the ends of the houses.

Pipe Frame

A pipe structure can be used to frame an air inflated greenhouse. Air is introduced into a chamber formed by two layers of four- or six-mil film.

The effect of the air under slight pressure is to force the inner layer of film over the circular greenhouse pipe frames. The outer layer assumes a circular shape over the frame and rides on a cushion of air.

The outer layer lifts three to four inches from the frame at the top and one to two inches from the frame at the foundation sill. Air enters the chamber through six-inch plastic tubing.

BEDS FOR GROWING SMALL PLANTS

Coldframes

A coldframe is a bottomless box with a removable top. It is used to protect small plants from wind and low temperatures. No artificial heat or manure is used inside a coldframe.

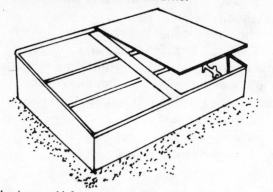

An aluminum cold frame glazed with corrugated fiberglass panels. Lightweight sash covers lift or slide for ventilation control.

Coldframes utilize the sun's heat. The soil inside the box is heated during the day and gives off its heat at night to keep the plants warm. The frame may be banked with straw or strawy manure to insulate it from the outside air and to retain heat.

With a coldframe, you can do many of the same things you do in a greenhouse. You can sow summer flowers and vegetables weeks before outdoor planting. Plants are protected from harsh weather and will grow to transplant size quickly. You can root cuttings of deciduous and evergreen shrubs and trees. Softwood cuttings of chrysanthemums, geraniums, and fuchsia, and leaf cuttings of rex begonias. African violets, and succulent and foliage plants take root faster in a coldframe, particularly during warmer months.

Portable coldframes can be built in your workshop from surplus materials you may have on hand. Coldframes are constructed from sections of

three- by four-foot or three- by six-foot millwork sash or plastic covered panels.

Hotbeds

A hotbed is a bed of soil enclosed in a glass or plastic frame. It is heated by manure, electricity, steam or hot-water pipes.

Hotbeds are used for forcing plants or for raising early seedlings.

Seeds may be started in a heated bed weeks or months before they can be sown out of doors. At the proper time the hotbeds can be converted into a coldframe for hardening. Then the plants may be moved to the garden when outdoor conditions are favorable.

Between ten and 15 watts of electric heat should be provided for every square foot of growing area in a hotbed.

If the bed is in a sunny, well-sheltered location, and the climate not too severe, ten watts per square foot should be adequate. Lining the side walls with moistureproof insulation is desirable. For localities with very cold winters, a higher heat capacity is needed. Fifteen watts per square foot is recommended.

Tape or wire screening, ¼- or ½-inch mesh, should be placed over the heating tape or cable to prevent possible damage by cultivating tools.

Do not place hotbed cables of any type directly in peat. When peat dries out it acts as an insulator and may cause the cable to overheat. Use a thermostat to control temperature automatically and make more efficient use of electricity.

Temperatures from 50 to 70 degrees Fahrenheit are best for hotbeds. On very cold nights cover the beds with mats, burlap, straw, or boards.

Weatherproof Wire

Use weatherproof wire for all outside wiring. Wire size depends upon the distance to be covered and the number of hotbeds to a circuit. Use approved terminal equipment and follow safe wiring practices. All wiring must conform to local wiring codes.

HEATING

Many types of heaters and heating systems are satisfactory for greenhouses.

Heating equipment can be a space heater, a forced-air heater, a hot-water or steam system, or electric heaters. Radiant heat lamps over plants and soil heating cable under plants can also be used.

Space heaters

For low-cost heating for small greenhouses, use one or more ordinary space heaters. WARNING: If you use a gas, oil, or coal heater, be sure to have a fresh air supply to avoid carbon monoxide buildup due to restricted oxygen supply. Fans are also needed to improve circulation. Use high grade (low sulfur) kerosene to avoid sulfur dioxide damage; the need for high ignition temperature to avoid carbon monoxide and ethylene buildup is important.

Forced-air heater

The best system for heating a small greenhouse is a forced-air furnace with a duct or plastic type system to distribute heat.

Hot-water or steam heater

A hot-water system with circulator or a steam system linked with automatic ventilation will give adequate temperature control.

Electric heaters

Overhead infrared heating equipment combined with soil cable heat provides a localized plant environment, which allows plants to thrive even though the surrounding air is at a lower than normal temperature. Electric resistance-type heaters are used as space heaters or in a forced air system.

VENTILATION

Even during cold weather a greenhouse can get too warm on bright, sunny days. So ventilation equipment should be built into your greenhouse to control temperatures in all seasons. If you use hand-operated roof vents, they will require frequent temperature checks.

Exhaust fans should be large enough to change the air in the greenhouse once every minute.

If the greenhouse is high enough, place the exhaust fan and the motorized intake louvers above the doors at opposite endwalls. This will exhaust the hottest, most humid air, and prevent a direct draft on the plants near the intake.

Fan and duct ventilation can also be used for automatic greenhouse heating and ventilation. Plastic ducts are suspended by wires or straps from the roof of the greenhouse. The fan-heater-louver unit gives positive air flow and the polyethylene duct distributes the incoming air.

SHADING YOUR GREENHOUSE

When protection from the sun is needed, use roll-up screens of wood or aluminum, vinyl plastic shading, or paint-on materials.

Roll-up screens are available with pulleys and rot-resistant nylon ropes.

Vinyl plastic shading is made of a flexible film that reduces light from 55 to 65 percent. The material comes in rolls and installs easily against the glass inside your greenhouse. To apply, just wash the glass with a wet sponge, then smooth the plastic onto the wet glass.

Shading compound can also be applied on the outside of glass greenhouses.

EVAPORATIVE COOLING

An evaporative cooler (or fan and pad system) eliminates excessive heat and adds beneficial humidity to the greenhouse atmosphere.

Warm air flows out through roof vents or exhaust fans. Temperature is lowered, humidity is increased, and watering needs are reduced.

The cooler must be installed outside the greenhouse. If it is inside, it can only humidify and cannot cool.

MIST PROPAGATION CONTROLS

Mist sprays are used in propagating to keep the atmosphere humid. There are two types of mist propagation controls.

Time clock system

This system of automatic watering includes:

A dual-time clock consisting of a 24-hour clock and a six-minute clock.

An electric water valve with strainer.

Hose bibbs.

A toggle switch to give you a choice of manual or automatic operations.

Evaporation system

This system provides a special unit that operates within the mist spray from the nozzles. When the stainless steel or ceramic screen and the plants become saturated, the screen tilts to a downward position, which switches off the water.

The water evaporates both on the mesh screen and on the cuttings. When the screen loses weight, the screen raises and actuates the switch. This opens the solenoid valve and starts the misting cycle again, according to the needs of the cuttings.

Because this control is activated by the weight of the water, it is fully automated.

CO_2 AND LIGHT CONTROL

Carbon dioxide (CO_2) and light are needed for plant growth. Closed greenhouses often have too little carbon dioxide during the day to effectively utilize available light. Therefore, plants grow poorly when air vents are closed.

Because light and carbon dioxide complement each other in plant growth, additional electric lights in greenhouses combined with good carbon dioxide control will increase yields.

CO_2 equipment utilizing infrared sensors are available for greenhouse owners who want to benefit from carbon dioxide enrichment with supplementary lighting.

Inexpensive color metric kits are also available for determining the CO_2 levels in your greenhouse.

LIGHTING, TEMPERATURE, AND CONTROL UNITS

Artificial light in greenhouses can be used in the following ways:

To provide high intensity light when increased plant growth is desired.

To extend the hours of natural daylight or to provide a night interruption to maintain the plants on long-day conditions.

Proper lighting not only extends the gardening day by enabling the gardener to work in the greenhouse during the dark evenings of winter and early spring, but it aids plant growth.

Fluorescent lamps have the advantage of high light efficiency with low heat. This type of lamp is the most widely used for supplemental light. It is available in a variety of colors but cool-white lamps are the most commonly used.

Incandescent lamps vary in size from 60 watts to 500 watts. They are used to extend daylength in greenhouses. The grower can vary footcandle levels by adjusting the spacing and mounting height.

High-intensity discharge (HID) lamps have a long life (5000 hours or more). The lamp has a high emission of light in the regions utilized by plants.

Light meters

Inexpensive light meters are available for measuring the light intensity in greenhouses. The most common light meters are calibrated in foot candles or lux (10.76 foot candles).

Temperature

As a gardener you will be concerned with two temperatures—the air temperature required in the greenhouse and the minimum outside temperature that your heating equipment must overcome.

For most plants, a night temperature of 60-65 degrees in the greenhouse is adequate. The general rule, however, is not to have a higher temperature than is necessary.

If you grow some plants that require a higher temperature than is provided in the greenhouse, use a propagating case or a warmed bench with thermostatically controlled warming cables to warm the air surrounding the plants.

Index

D-E-F

G-H-I